THE SHANKILL

Photographs by Julie McCarthy | Introduction by Tony Macaulay

Daylight

Publisher: Michael Itkoff
Creative Director: Ursula Damm
Copy Editor: Gabrielle Fastman

ISBN: 978-1-954119-43-7

Printed by Ofset Yapimevi, Turkey

Daylight Books
E-mail: info@daylightbooks.org
Web: www.daylightbooks.org

The Shankill is a portrait of a resilient and tight-knit community along the Shankill Road in Belfast, Northern Ireland. Historically associated with the city's Protestant and Loyalist population, this neighborhood endured decades of sectarian violence during the Troubles. Though peace was formally declared in 1998 with the signing of the Good Friday Agreement, the conflict's legacy remains etched into the physical and emotional landscape.

At first glance, the Shankill feels familiar, lined with shops and greengrocers, humming with everyday life. But the past is ever present. Murals honoring fallen Loyalist figures abound, and a barrier known as a peace wall still separates the Shankill from its Catholic neighbors in West Belfast. This is a place where history hangs in the air, suspended between memory and an uncertain future.

The residents of the Shankill are eager to move beyond the shadows of the past. They no longer wish to be defined by the conflict alone. Instead, they embrace long-standing cultural traditions, such as lighting bonfires each July 12 to commemorate the Battle of the Boyne, and hosting parades honoring King William of Orange and the Orange Order. These rituals, while steeped in history, serve as affirmations of identity and belonging. Yet many fear their significance is slipping away in an increasingly globalized world.

I spent years photographing and listening in the Shankill, slowly becoming immersed in its rhythm and story. This is not just a story of survival, but of pride, connection, and the struggle to preserve selfhood amidst change. The experiences of the Shankill echo those of marginalized communities everywhere: voices often overlooked; histories misunderstood. Through these photographs, I hope to amplify one of those voices, and share a story of strength, solidarity, and home.

—Julie McCarthy

THE SHANKILL

I was a paperboy up the Shankill, so I was. The dates of my employment were 1975–1977. As a twelve-year-old, I delivered forty-eight *Belfast Telegraphs* every night, around the streets of Ballygomartin at the top of the Shankill Road. At a tumultuous time in the history of Belfast, I had the great responsibility of delivering the daily news of bombs and bullets to my discerning customers.

Since then, I've lived in different places, worked in various jobs, and written many books. However, because of my memoir *Paperboy: An Enchanting True Story of a Belfast Paperboy Coming to Terms with the Troubles* (HarperCollins, 2011), I'm most well known for being a wee paperboy up the Shankill. It's not unusual for strangers to come up to me in the street or in a café in Belfast and say, "What about ye, paperboy?" Last year, I was standing at a bus stop in Douglas, on the Isle of Man, when a gentleman approached me and asked, "Are you the paperboy?" Once I recovered from the shock, he explained that he, too, had grown up in the Shankill community in the 1970s. When this happens, one of the reasons I'm delighted is because I love where I come from—the people and the place.

The Shankill community starts near Belfast city center and stretches up to the hills that overlook West Belfast. It's one of the oldest roads in the city. The name Shankill derives from the Irish "seanchill," meaning "old church," referring to an ancient church site in the area dating back to the fifth century. The oldest maps of Belfast show the Shankill as a rural pathway with a church, connecting Belfast to the surrounding countryside. The Road (as locals call it!) became urbanized during the nineteenth century with Belfast's industrial boom.

Over the next one hundred years, the Shankill developed as a working-class district with a population, like my family, mainly employed in the engineering, linen, and shipbuilding industries. Rows and rows of two-up-two-down red brick terraced houses were constructed to accommodate the growing workforce, and many Protestants and Unionists from rural areas of Ulster and Scotland, with a strong loyalty to Britain, migrated to this part of the growing city of Belfast. In the late nineteenth century, my family, like many others, moved from County Antrim and settled in the Shankill. The terraced house where my great-grandparents lived still stands in Eccles Street.

During the twentieth century, the Shankill became iconic of the sectarian divisions in Belfast, separated from our neighbors on the Catholic and Nationalist Falls Road by a so-called "peace wall." Some of my family lived in the streets that used to run between the Shankill and the Falls, where Catholics and Protestants once lived side by side. At the outbreak of the Troubles in 1969, those streets became unsafe and were eventually demolished and replaced with barriers to keep our people apart. In the years that followed, the Shankill community suffered enormously from sectarian violence, paramilitarism, industrial decline, poor redevelopment, and persistent social, educational, and economic neglect. Despite all the hardships of history, the Shankill has endured with a distinctive sense of identity, culture, and community.

Back when I was a paperboy, I escaped from the grim realities of the Belfast streets into science fiction. One of my favourite television shows was *Doctor Who* on BBC1, where an alien timelord from the planet Gallifrey traveled through time and space in the TARDIS, his spaceship, which was disguised as an old blue English police box. One of the most thrilling parts of Doctor Who's adventures was that his TARDIS was bigger on the inside than the outside, and I believe the Shankill is the same!

From the outside, the Shankill can appear two-dimensional and stereotypically harsh, poor, hard-line, and sectarian. From the inside it's more multidimensional, more nuanced and diverse. Different parts of the Shankill have different identities: Lower Shankill, Mid Shankill, and Upper Shankill. There are different groups and outlooks within the community. This diversity includes different businesses, churches, an iconic library, Loyalist marching bands, women's groups, community groups, peacebuilding and youth groups (often twinned with groups on the Falls Rd.), the Orange Order, sports clubs, primary schools, nurseries, charities, arts and music groups, newcomers from different cultures, some people learning the Irish language, and many people who celebrate Ulster Scots traditions. The Shankill Road is a community like any other, with its own joys, struggles, and humanity. Like most working-class communities, the Shankill is full of a mixture of talent, toughness, warmth, humor, and creativity.

The rare beauty of this book is Julie McCarthy's stunning photography of the faces of people on the Shankill. Every face tells its own story. You can see joy and sorrow, belief and conviction, resilience and struggle, hope and celebration. Here you will see all of this and more on the faces of the people of the Road. As you study this thoughtful and remarkable collection of photographs, I hope you will find connection and insight into the community I love, which is bigger on the inside than the outside, so it is.

Tony Macaulay
January 2025

Dr. Tony Macaulay is an author, peacebuilder, and broadcaster. His Irish bestselling memoirs of growing up in the Shankill community during the Troubles, Paperboy, Breadboy, *and* All Growed Up, *have been adapted into hit musicals at the Lyric Theatre in Belfast. His autobiography* Little House on the Peace Line *tells the story of how he lived and worked on the Belfast peace line in the 1980s. His debut novel,* Belfast Gate, *was Book of the Week in the* Irish News. *His latest novel,* Kill the Devil: A Love Story from Rwanda, *was co-authored with Rwandan screenwriter Juvens Nsabimana. He was awarded an honorary doctorate by Ulster University for services to literature and peacebuilding at home and abroad.*

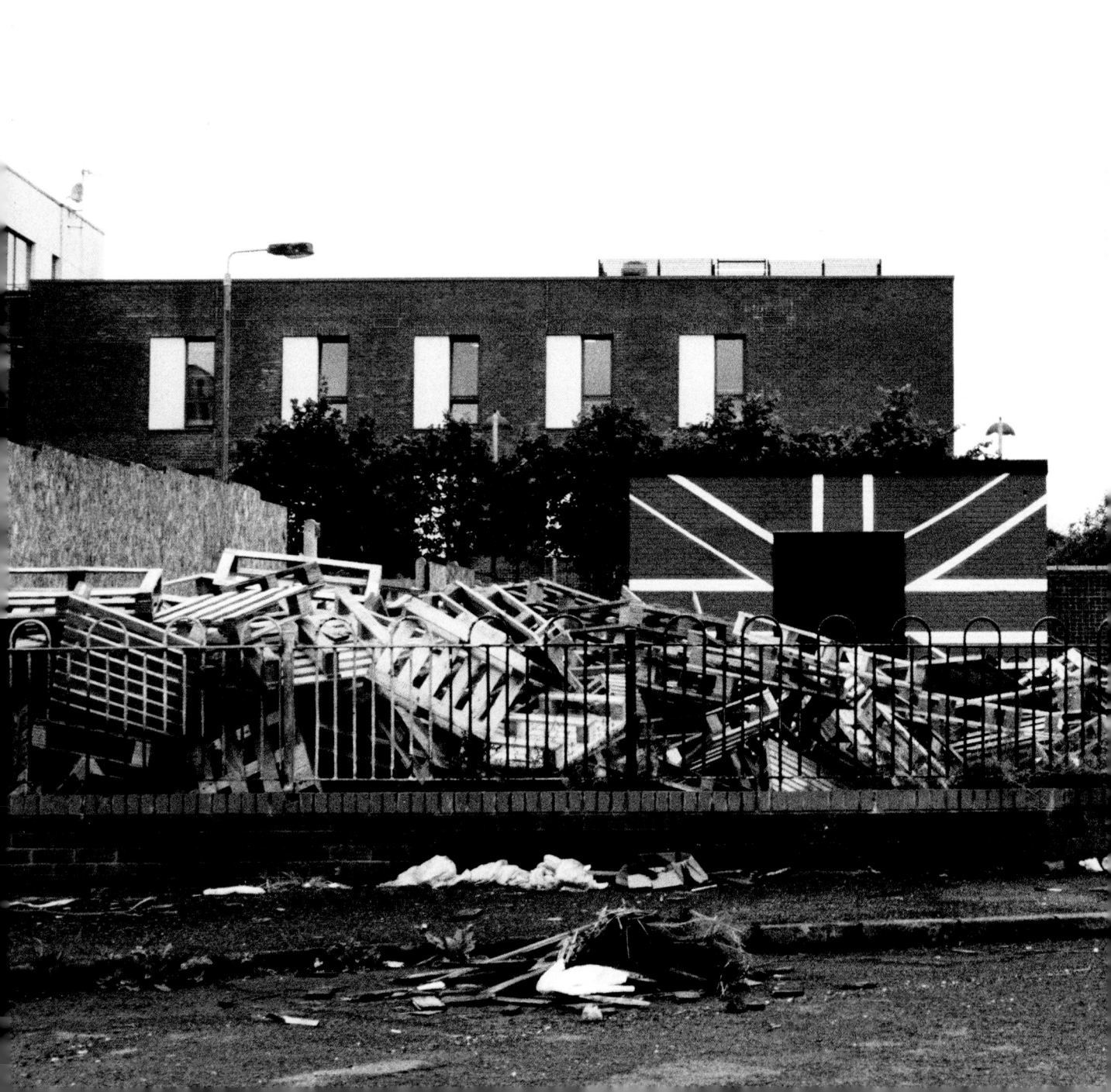

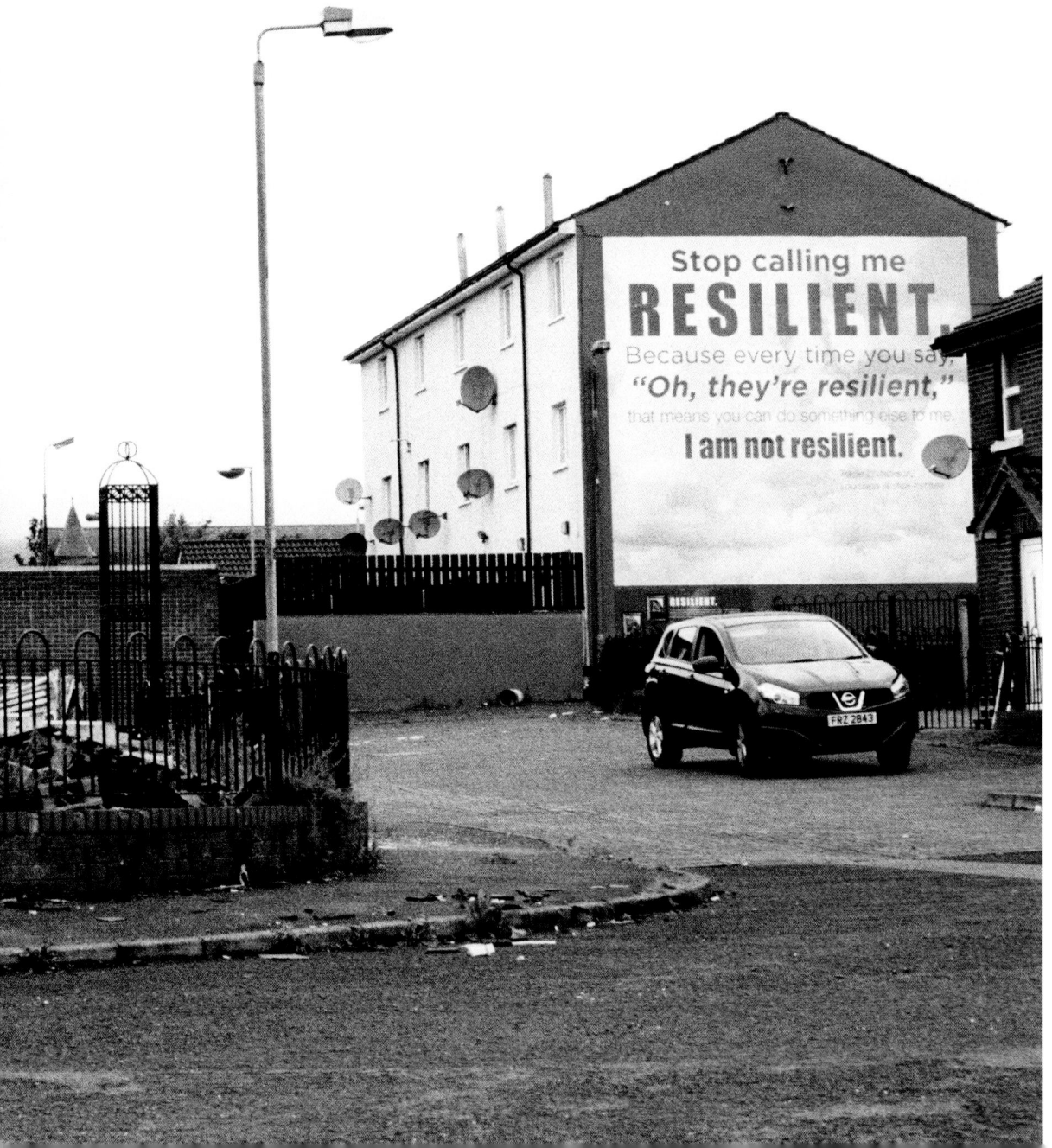

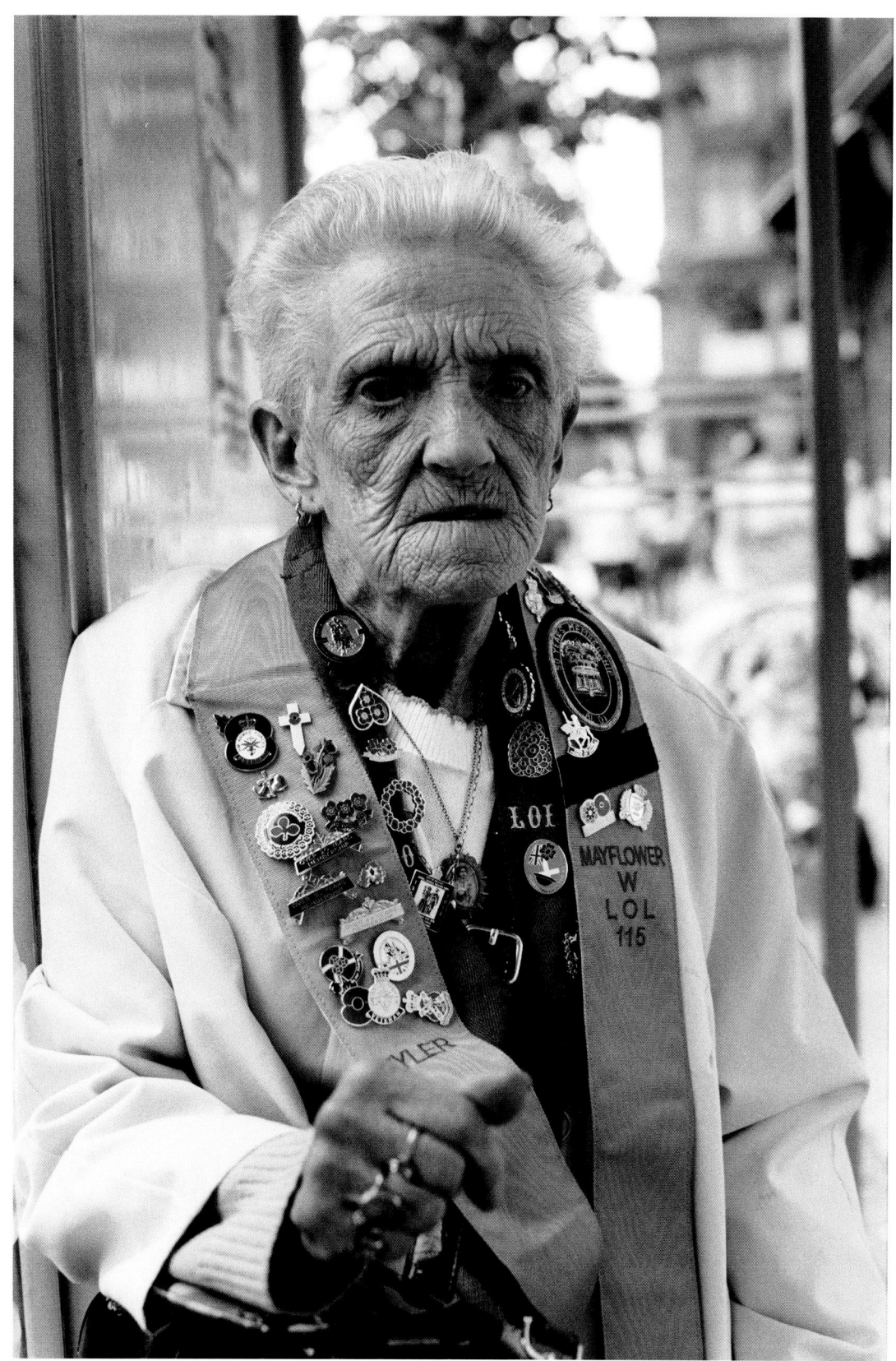

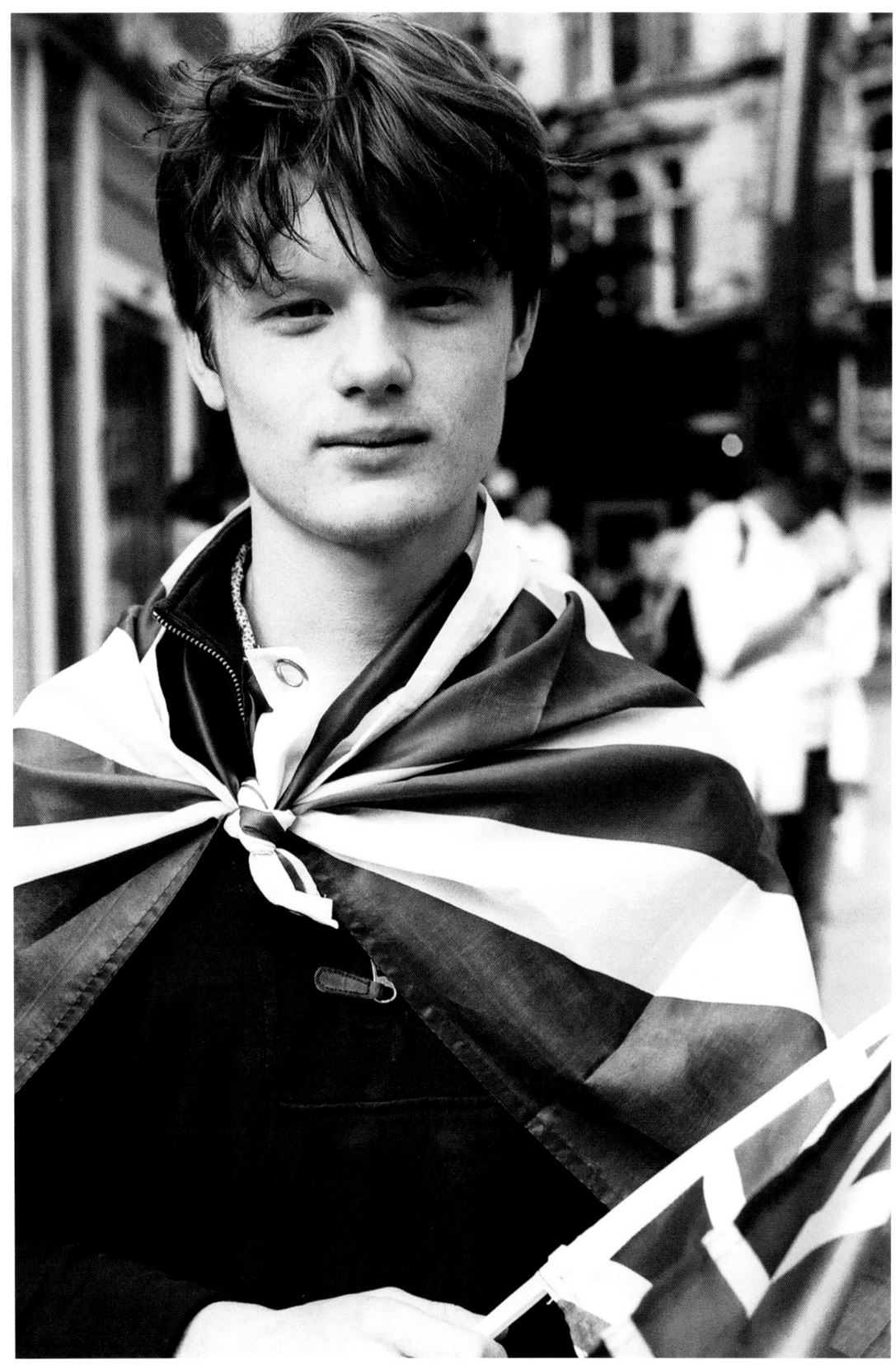

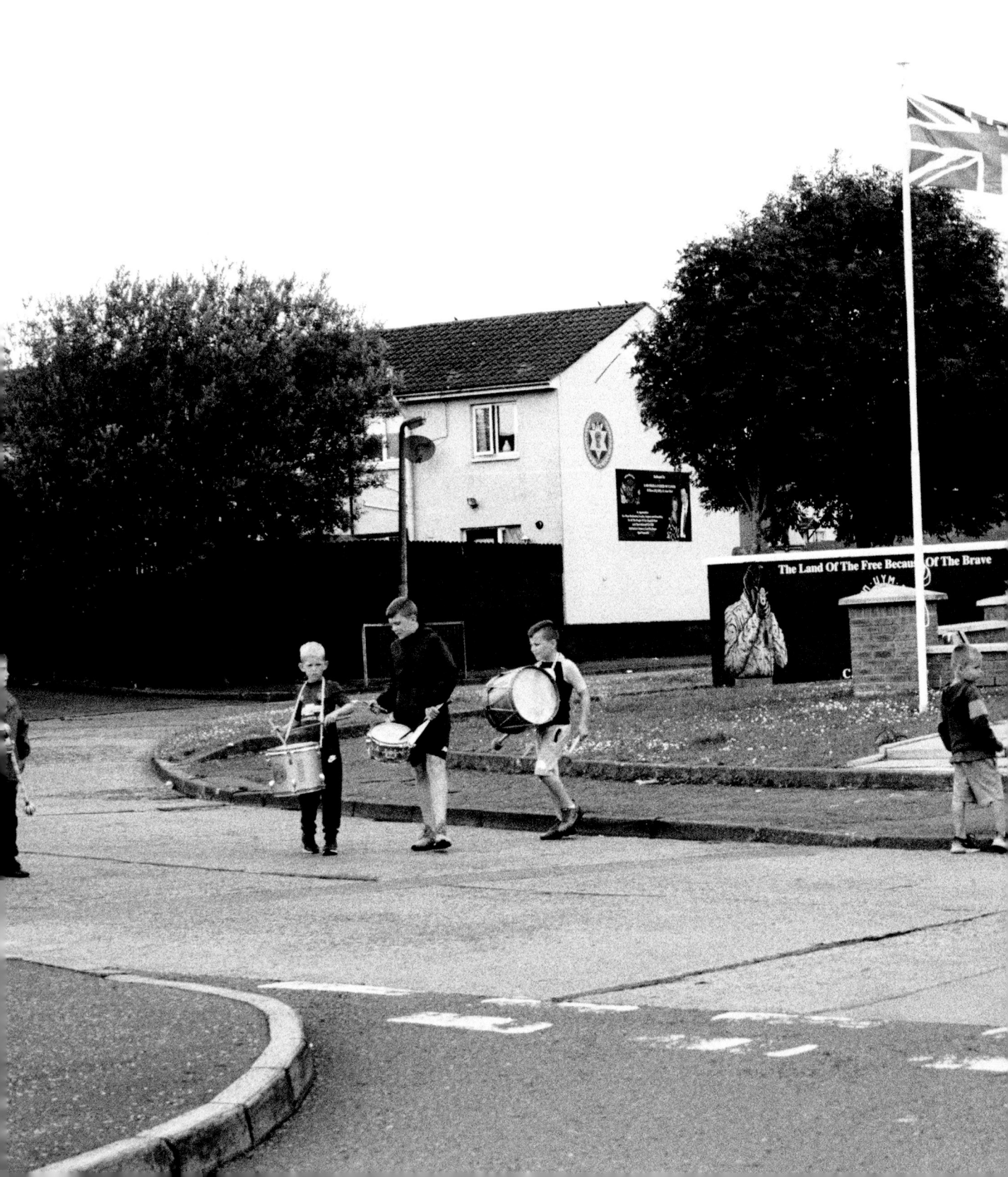

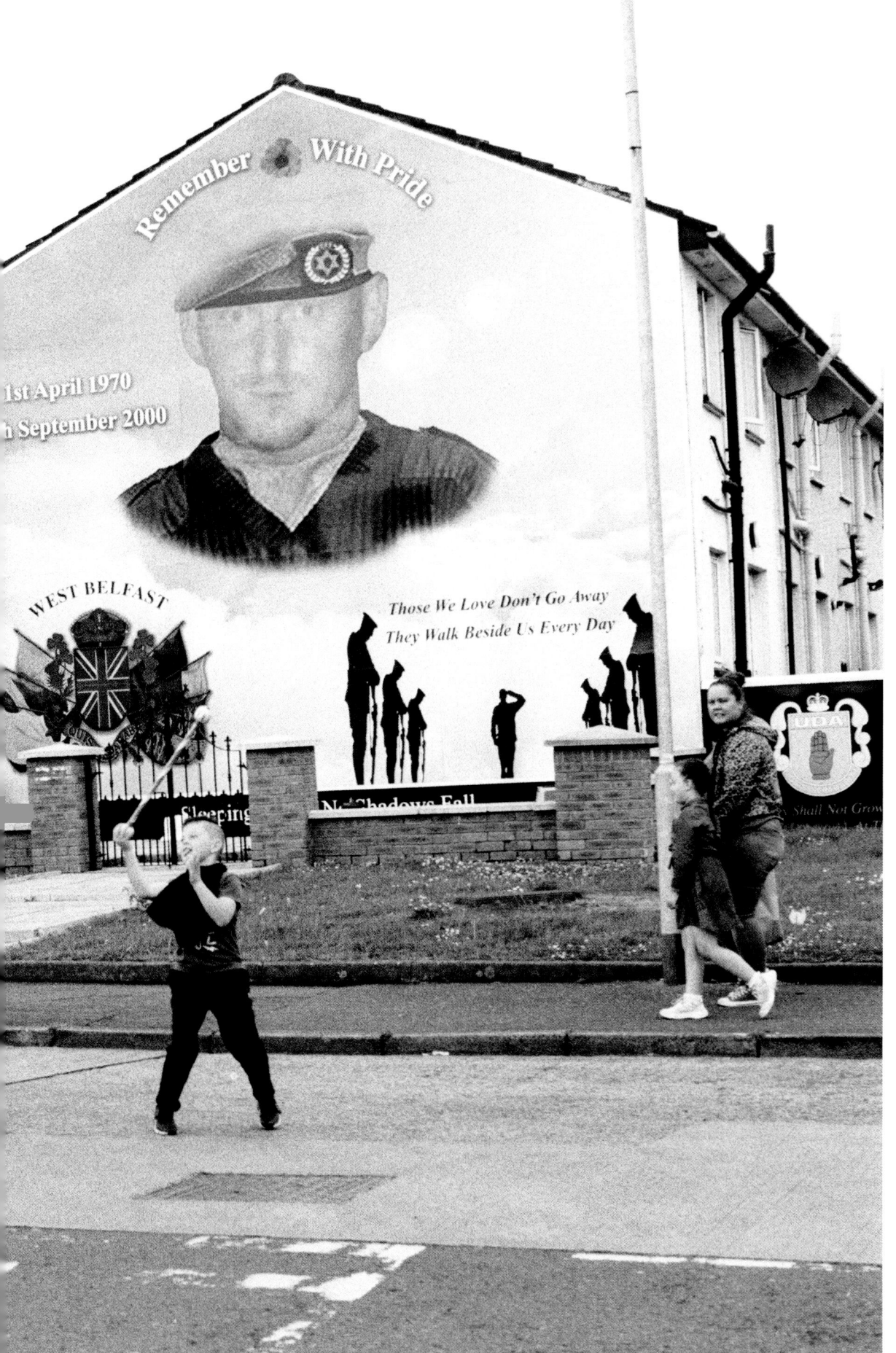

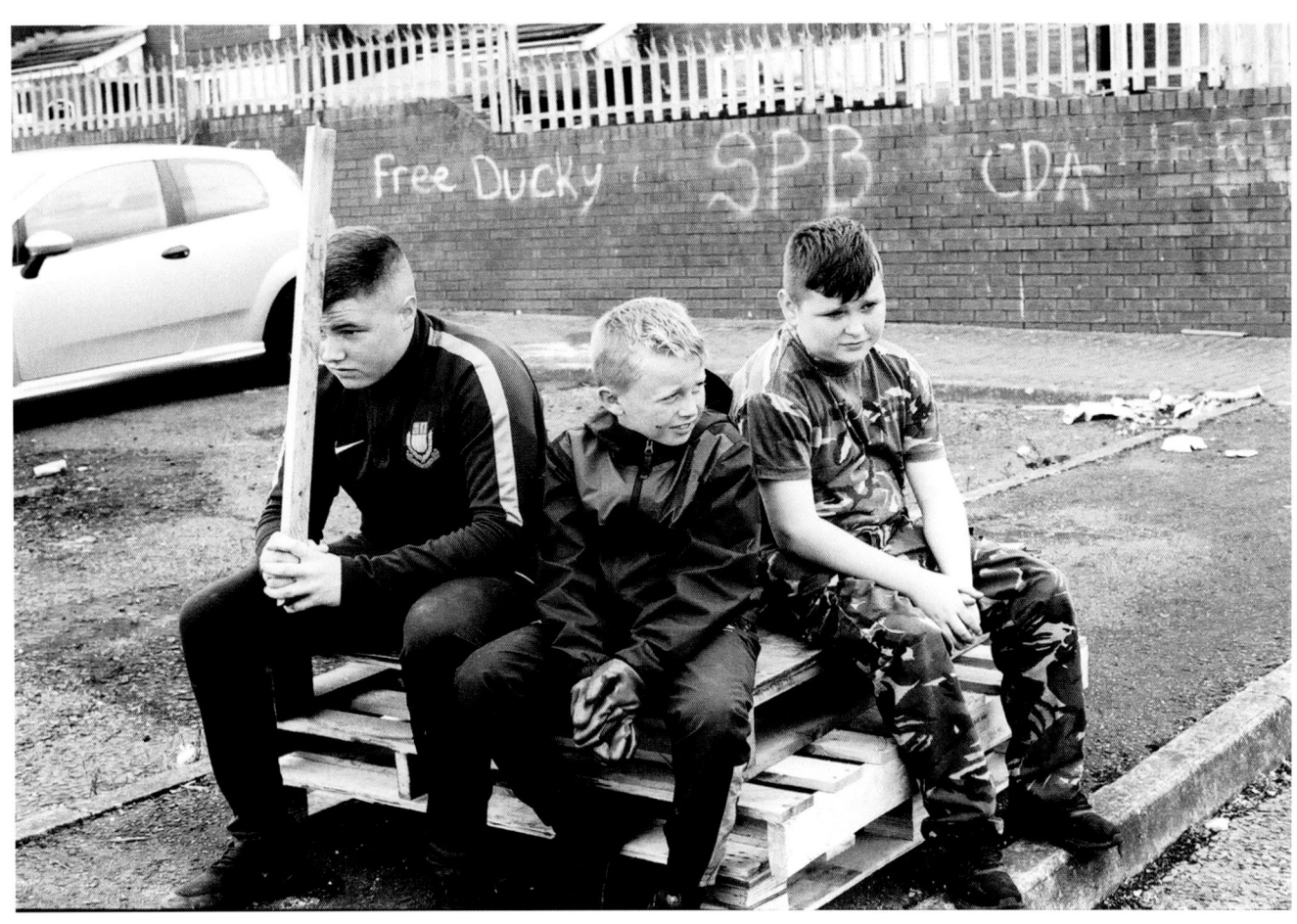

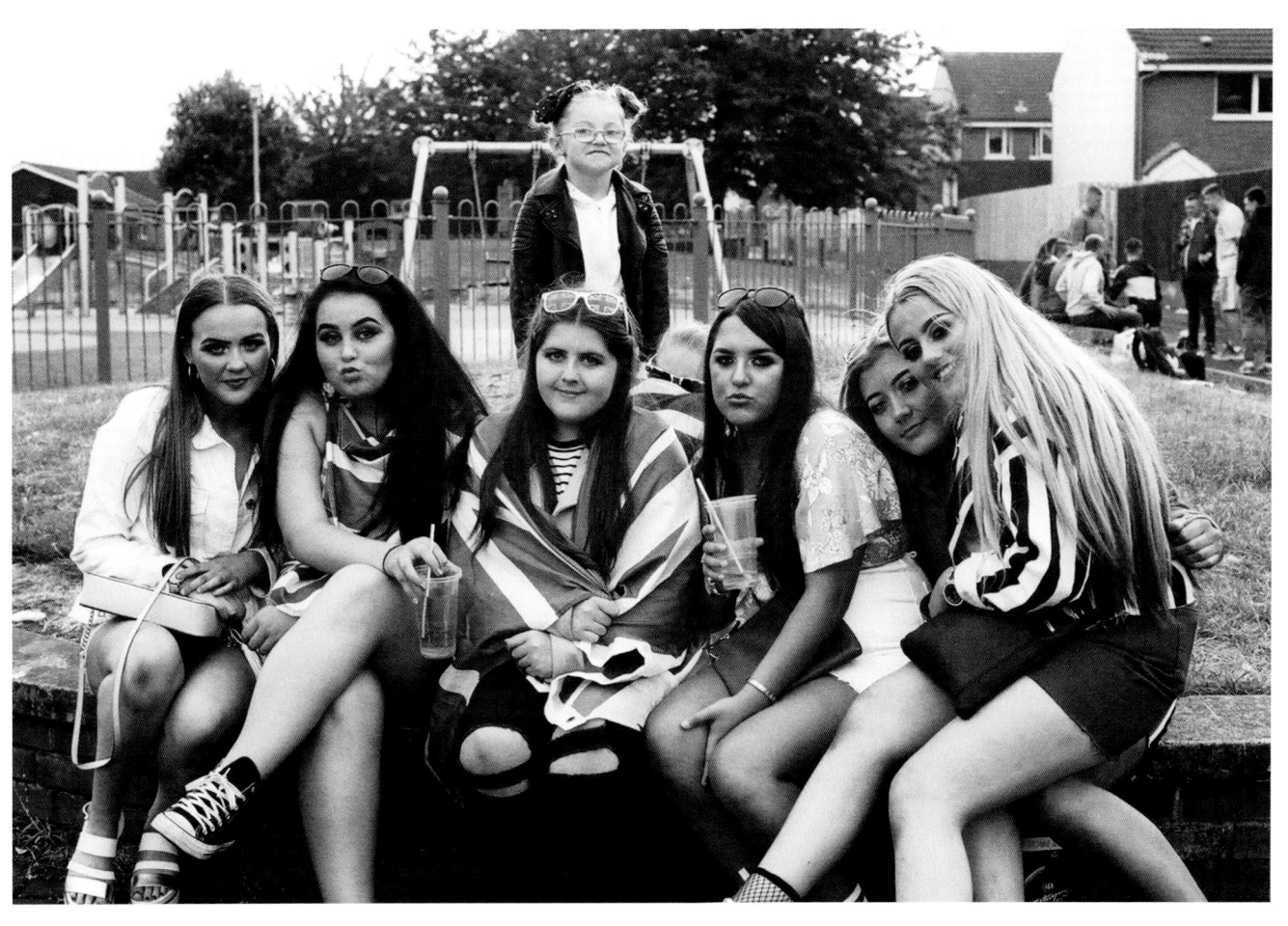

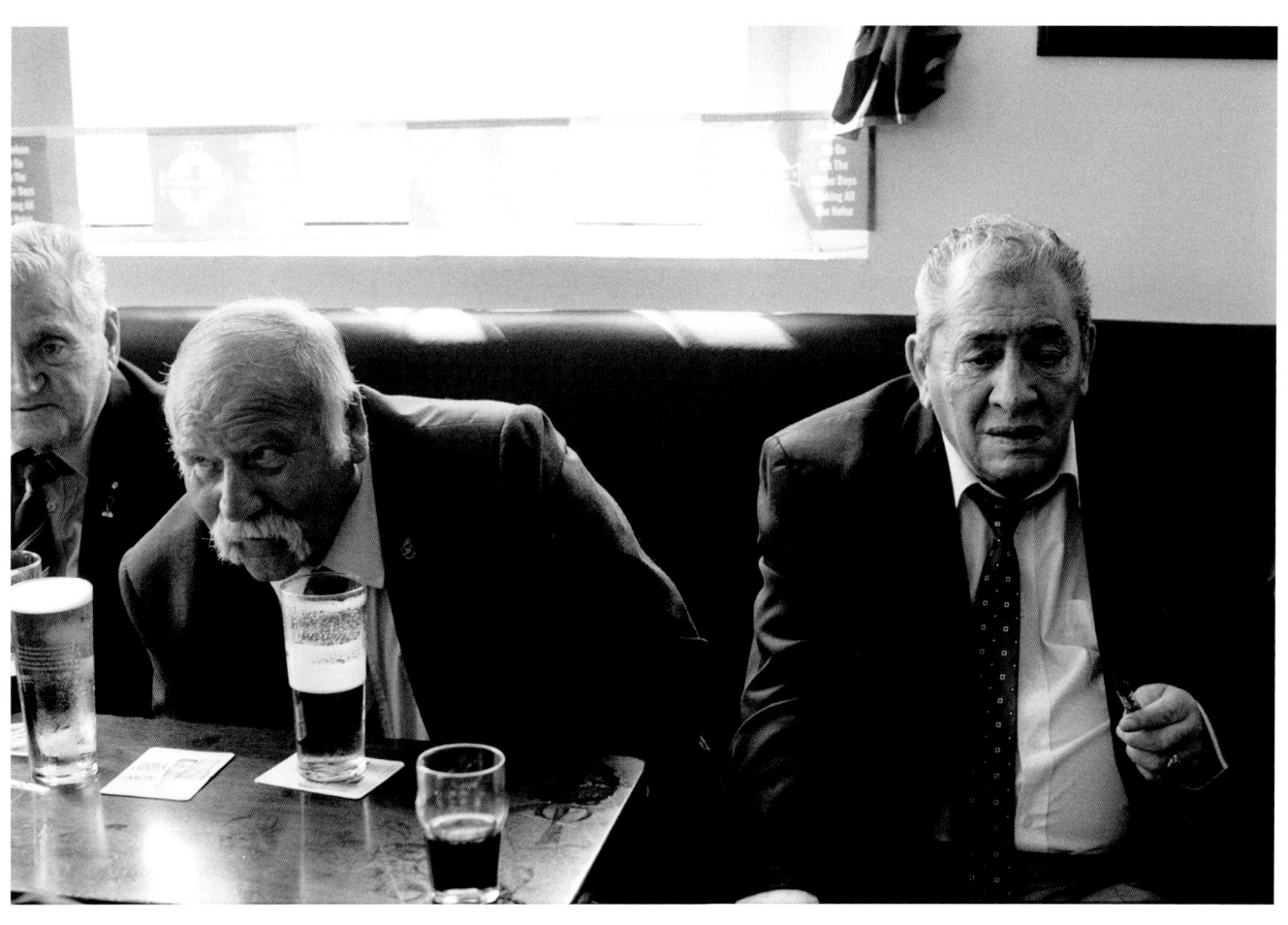

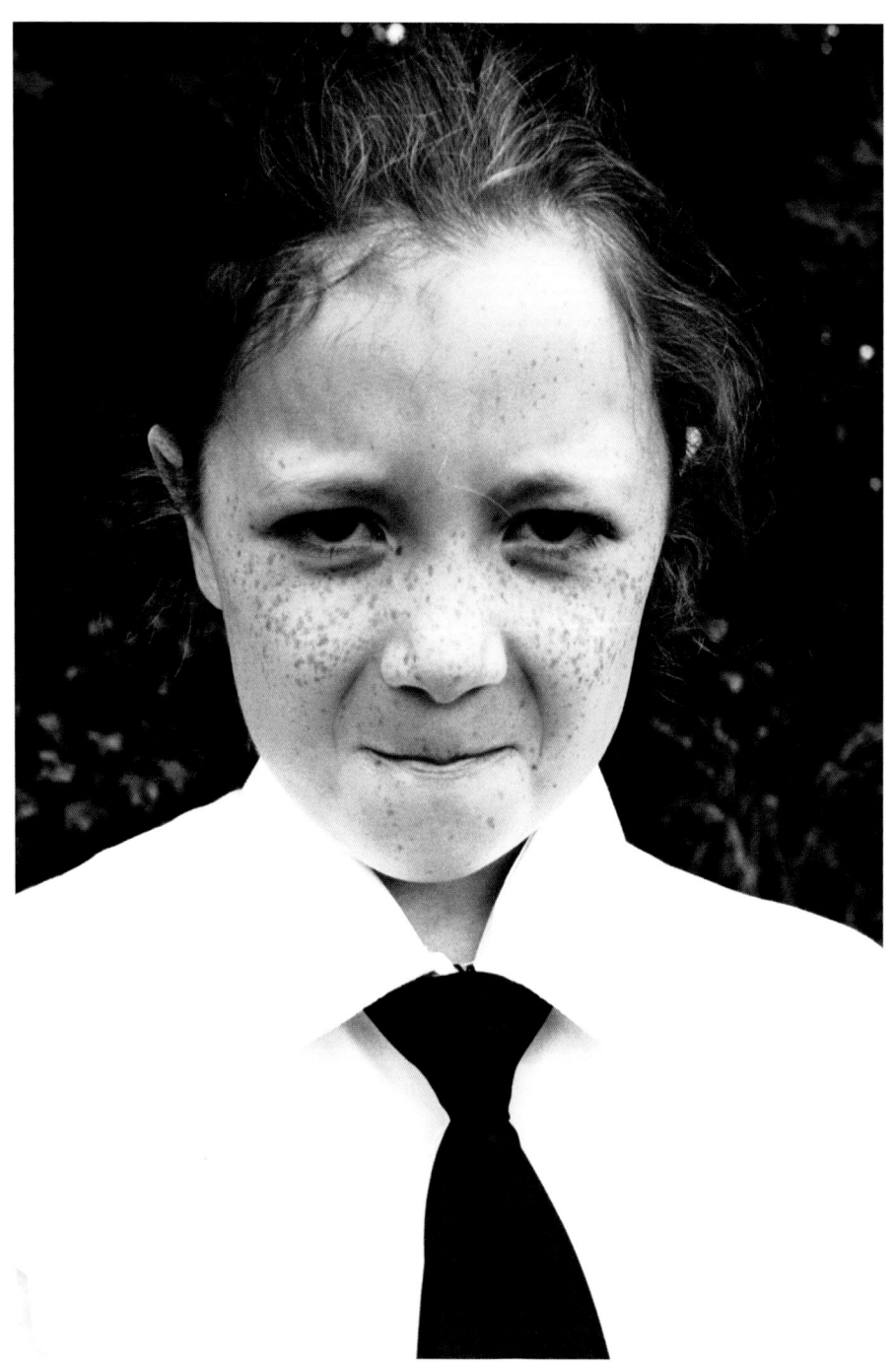

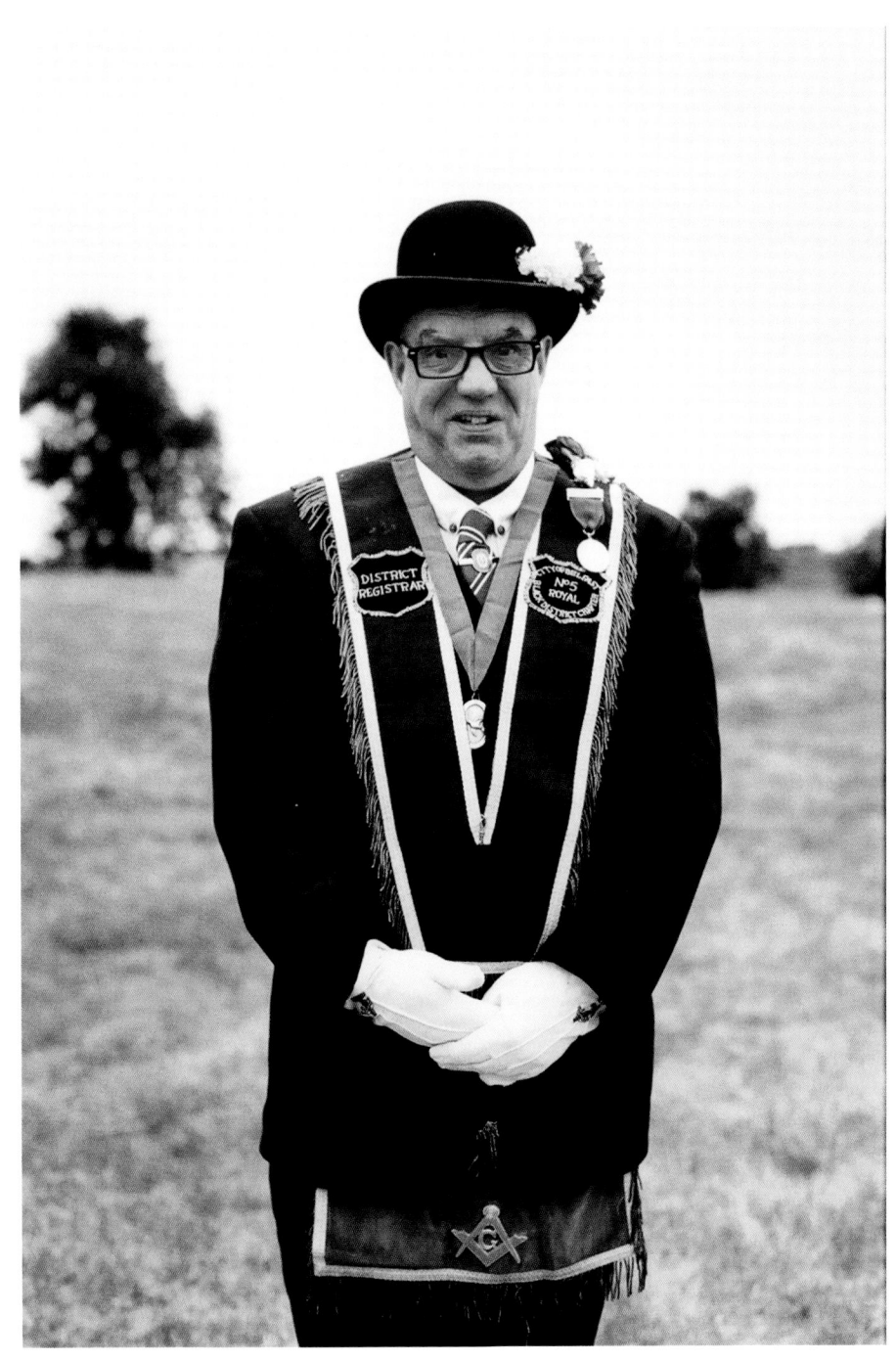

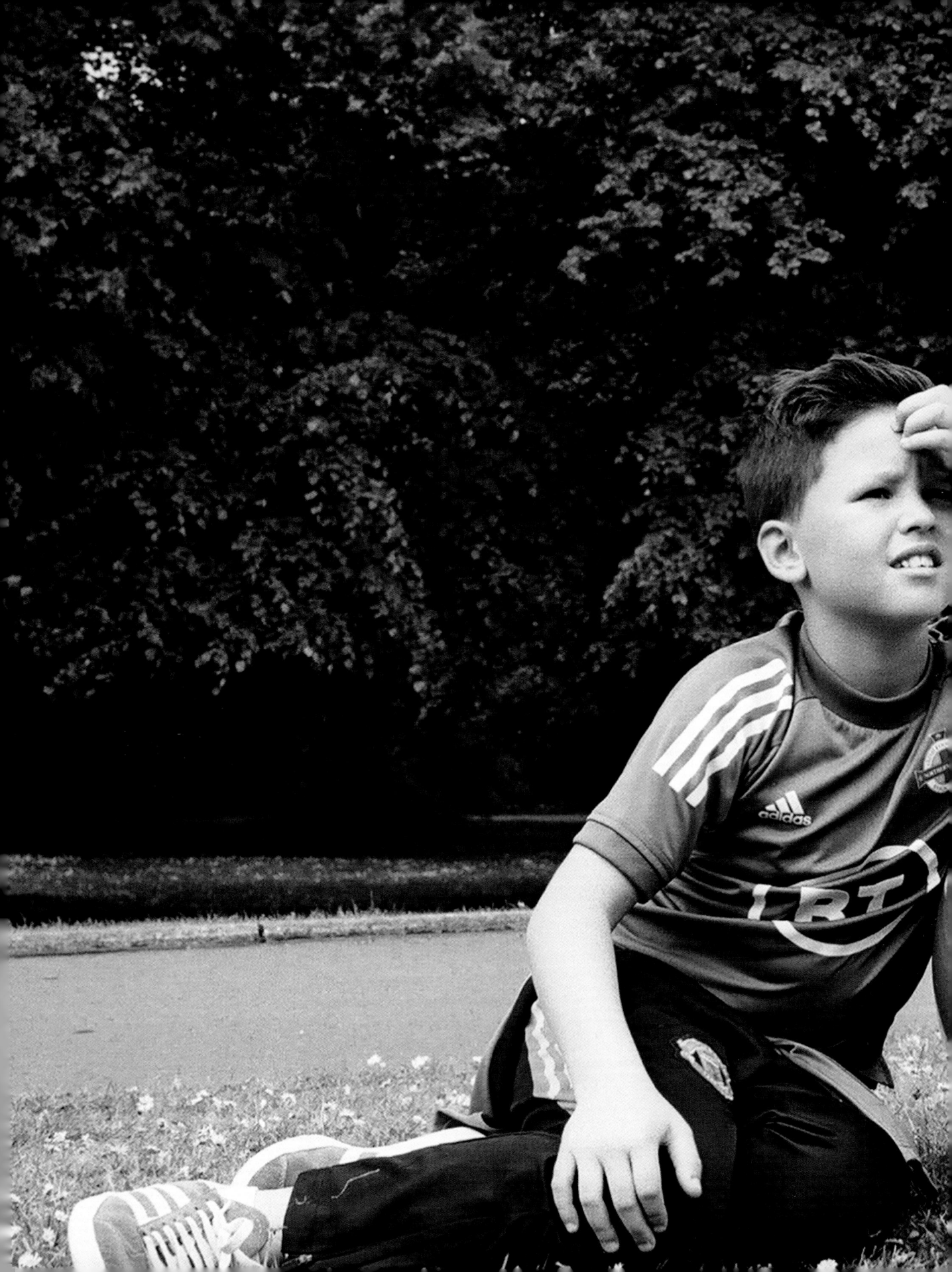

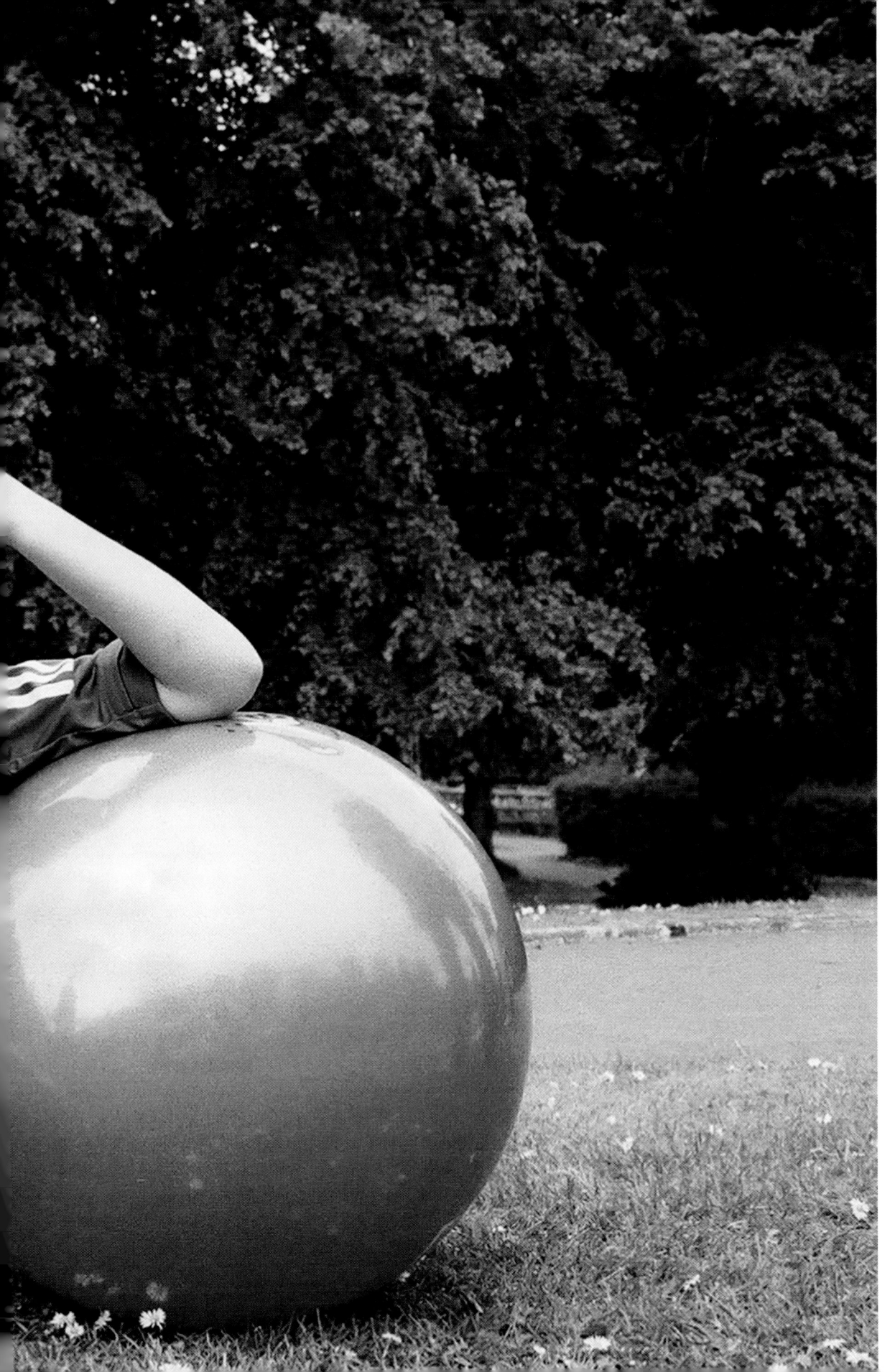

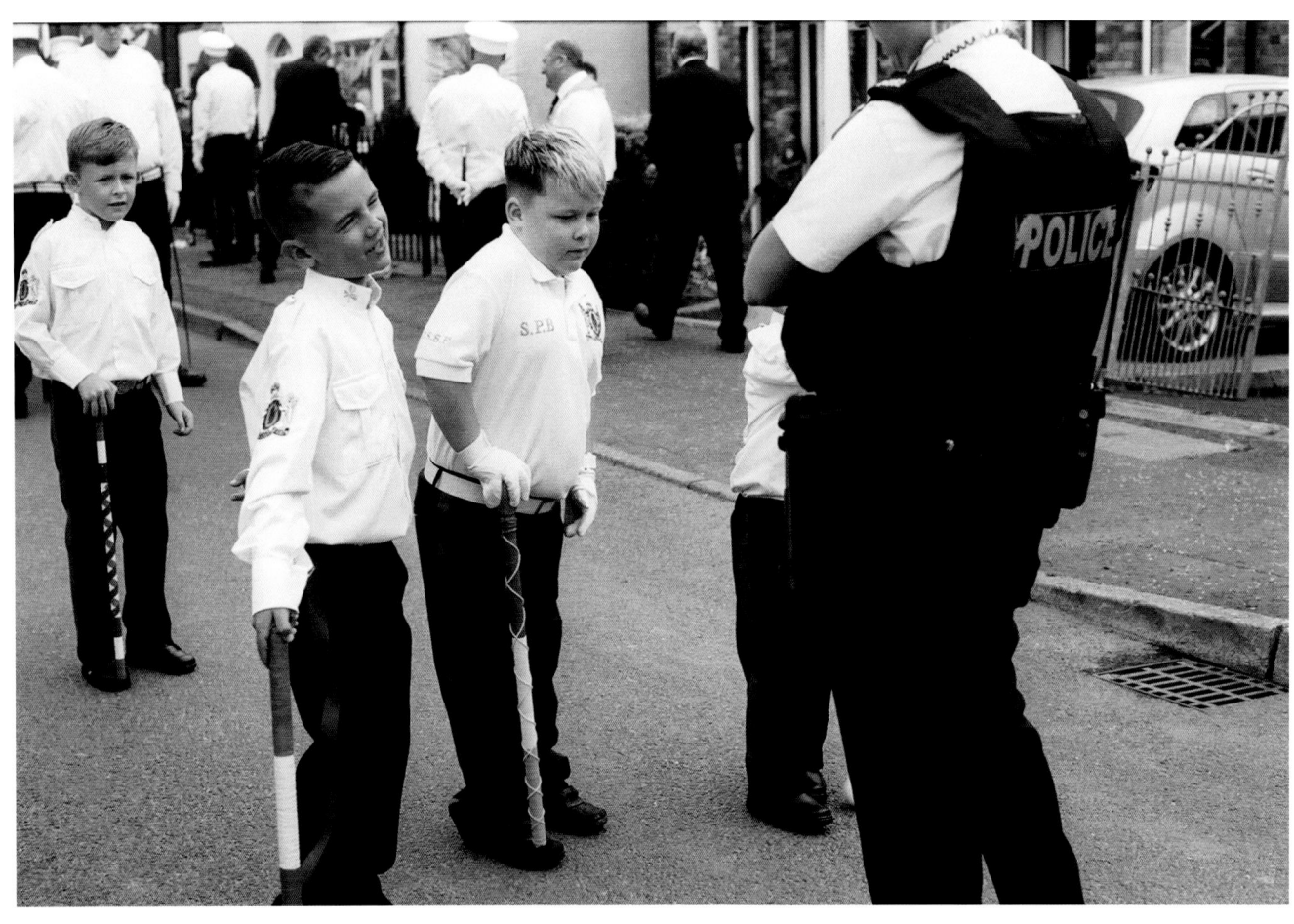

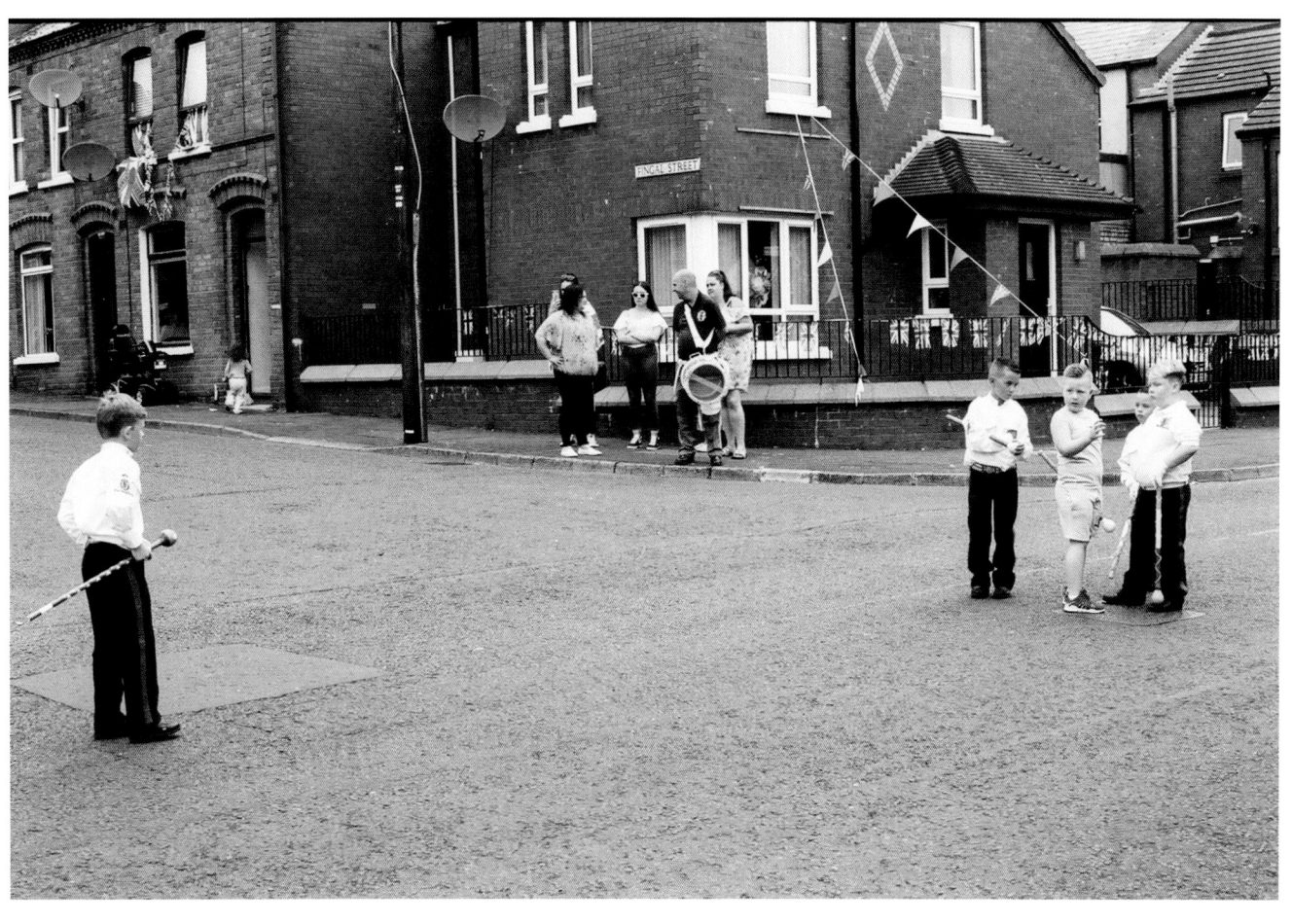

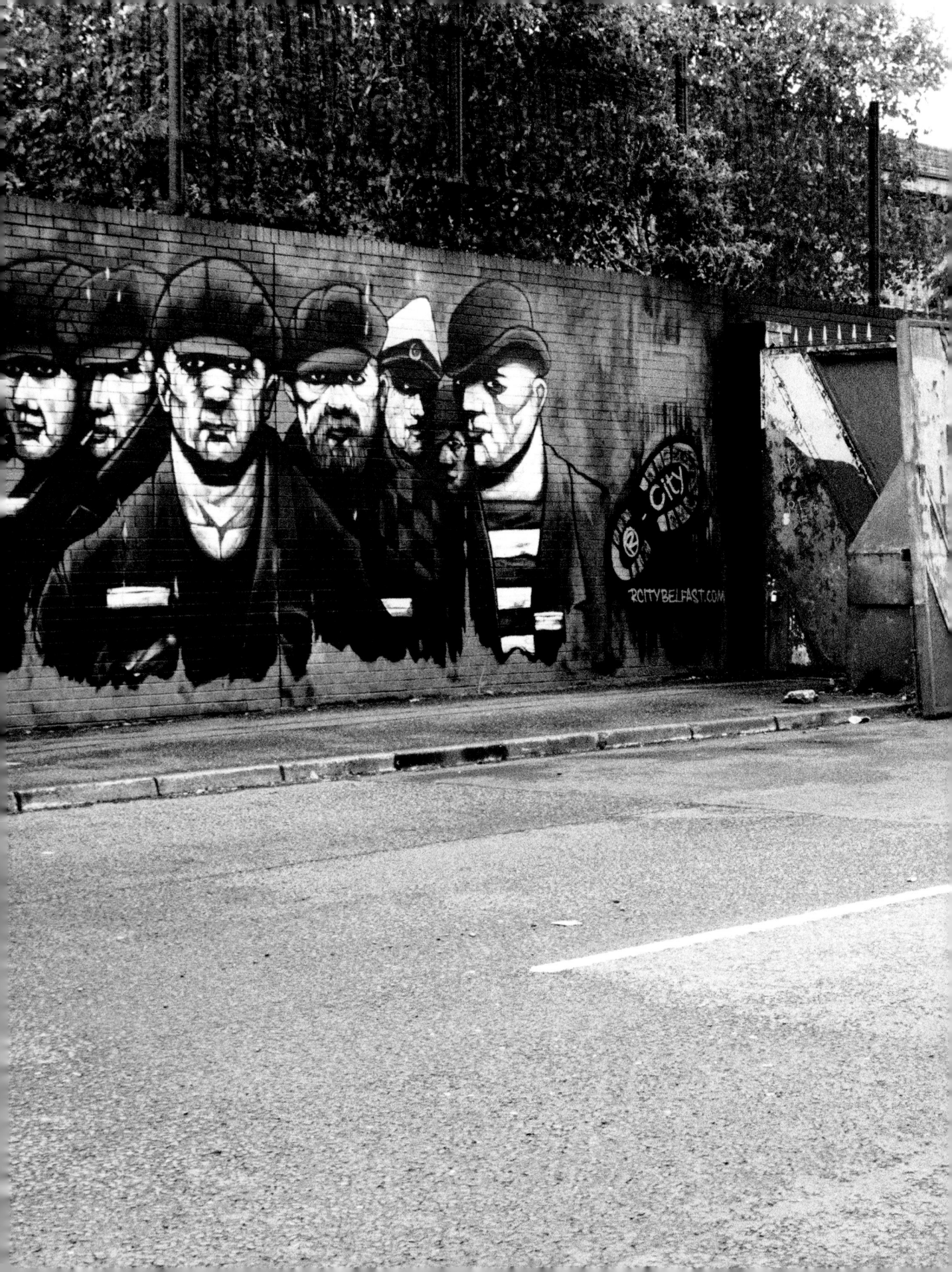

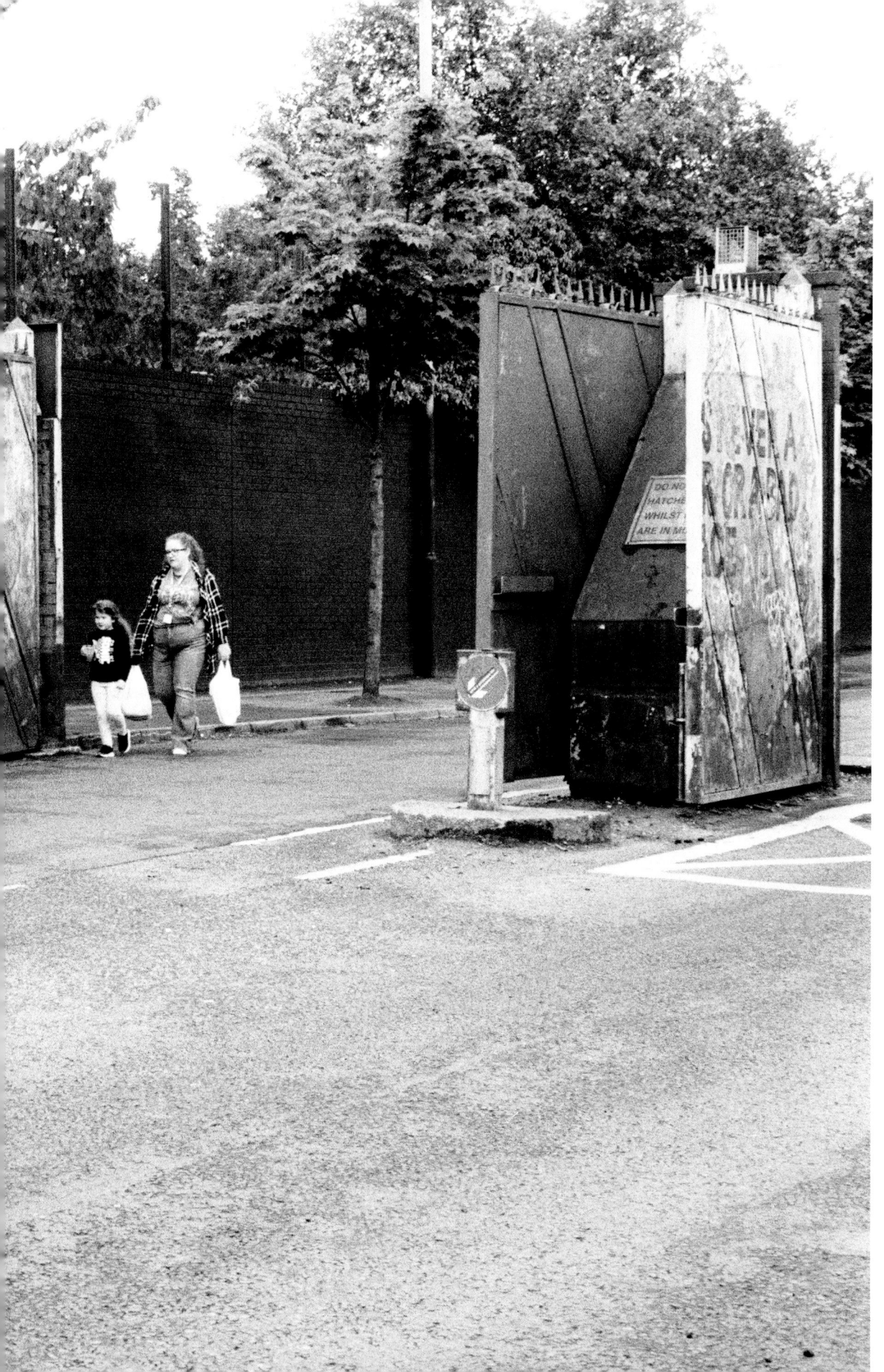

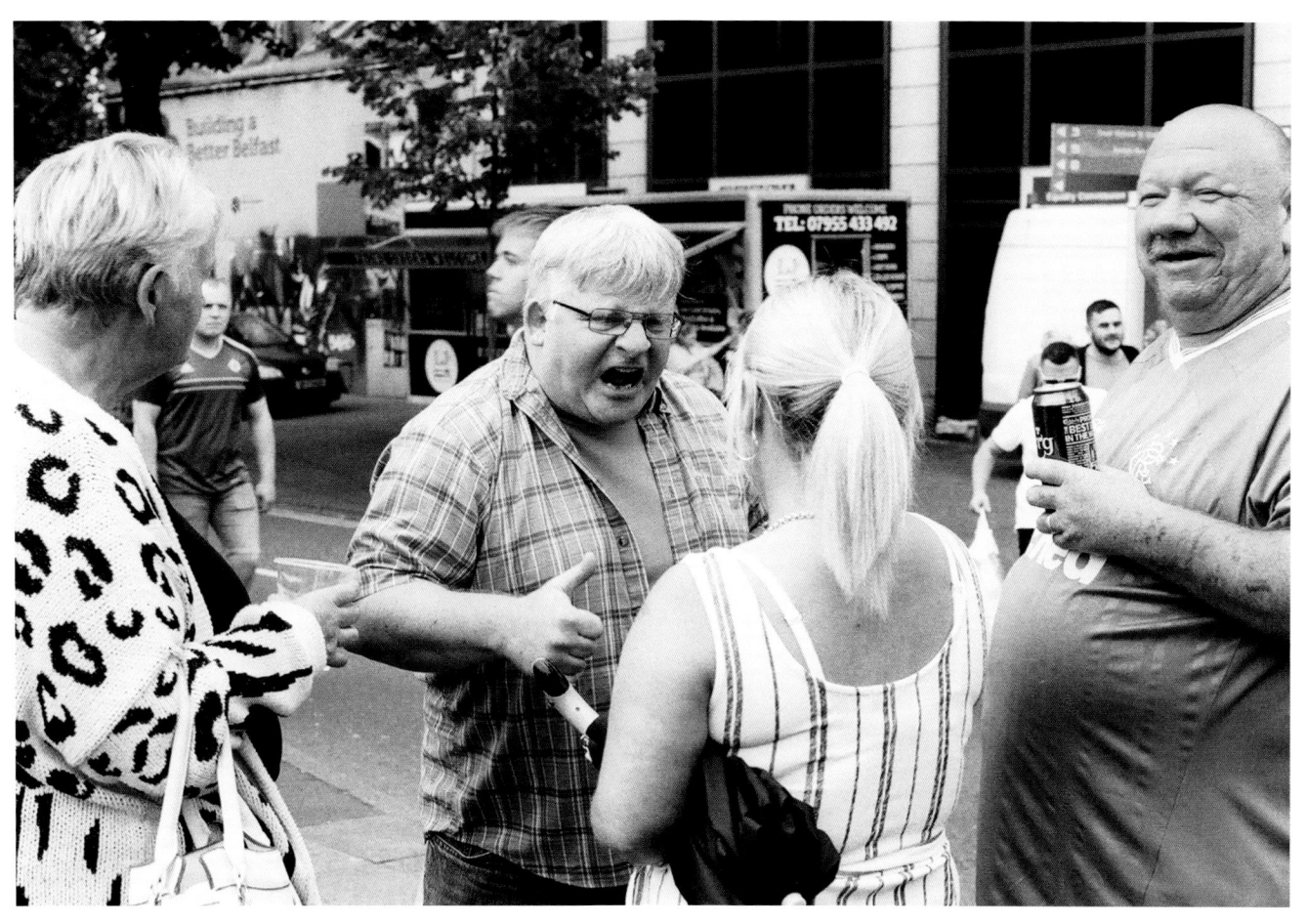

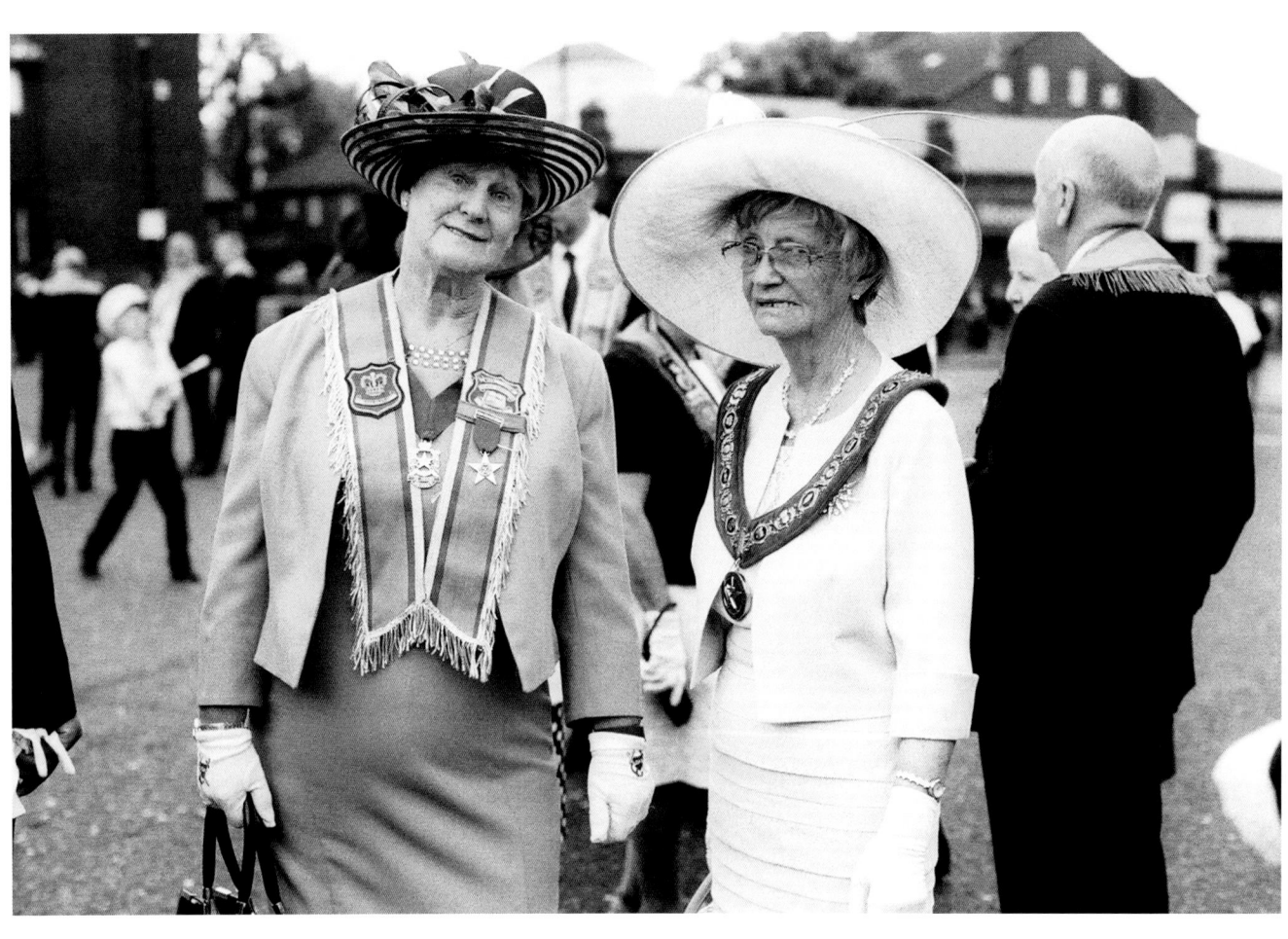

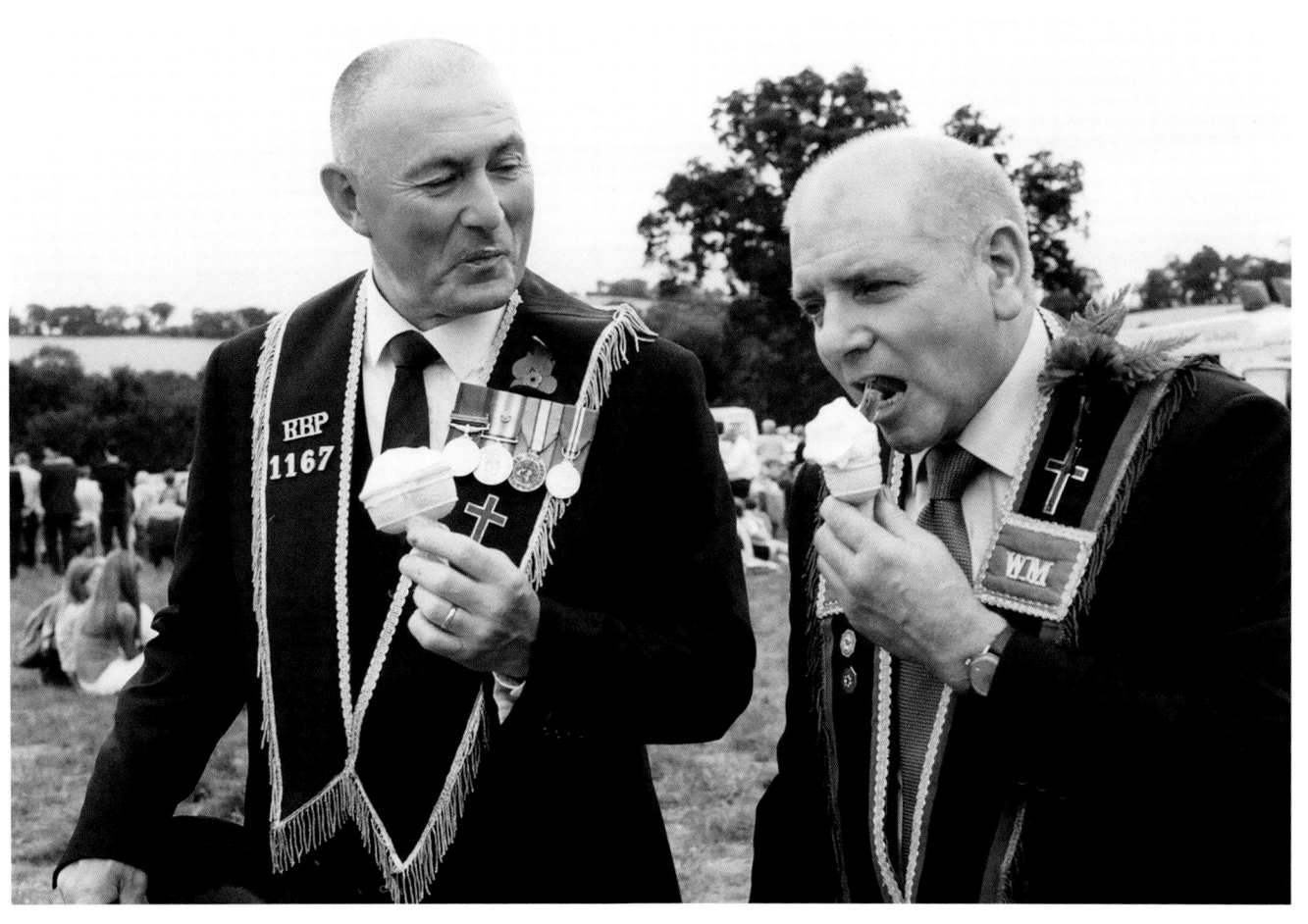

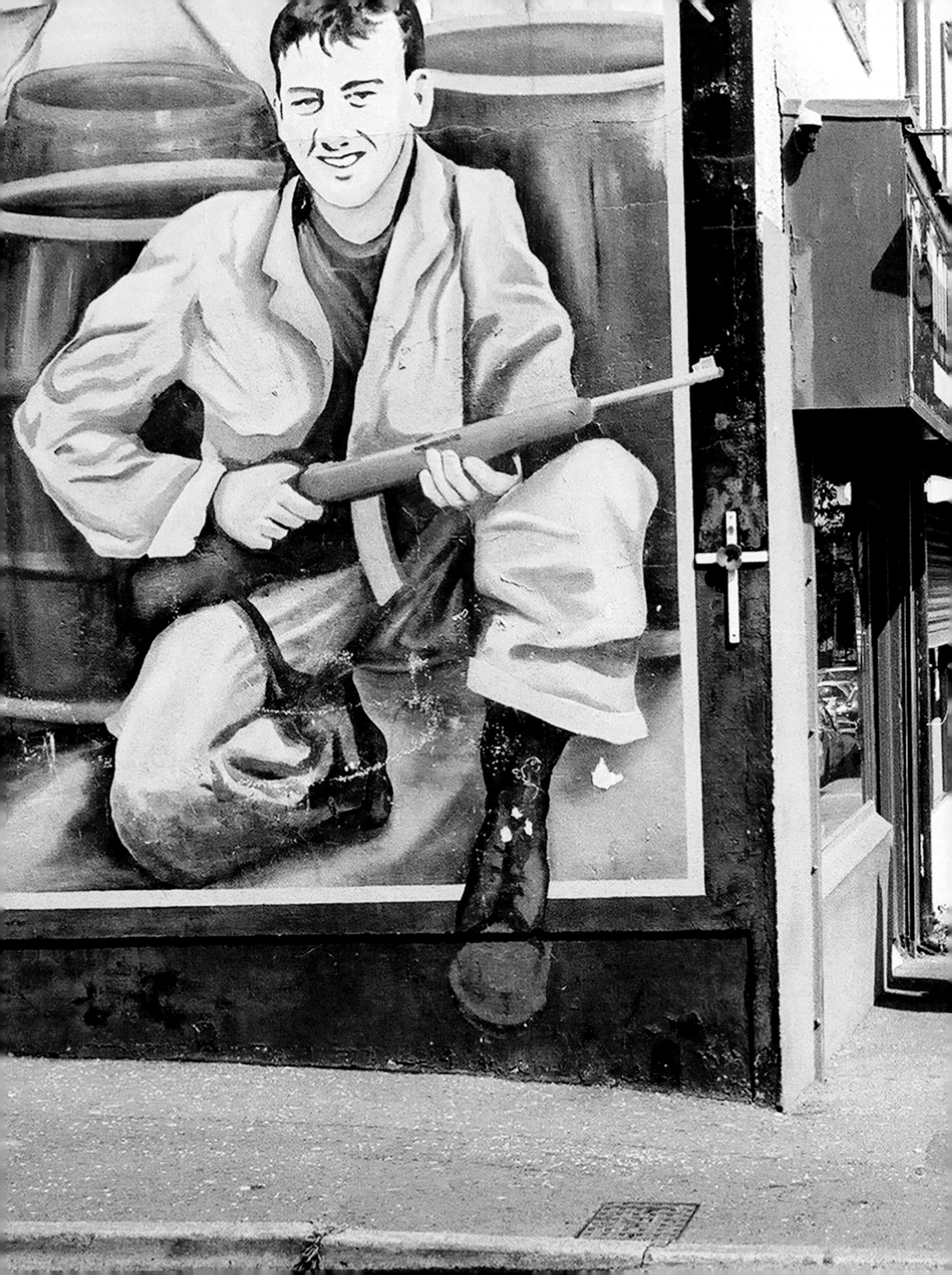

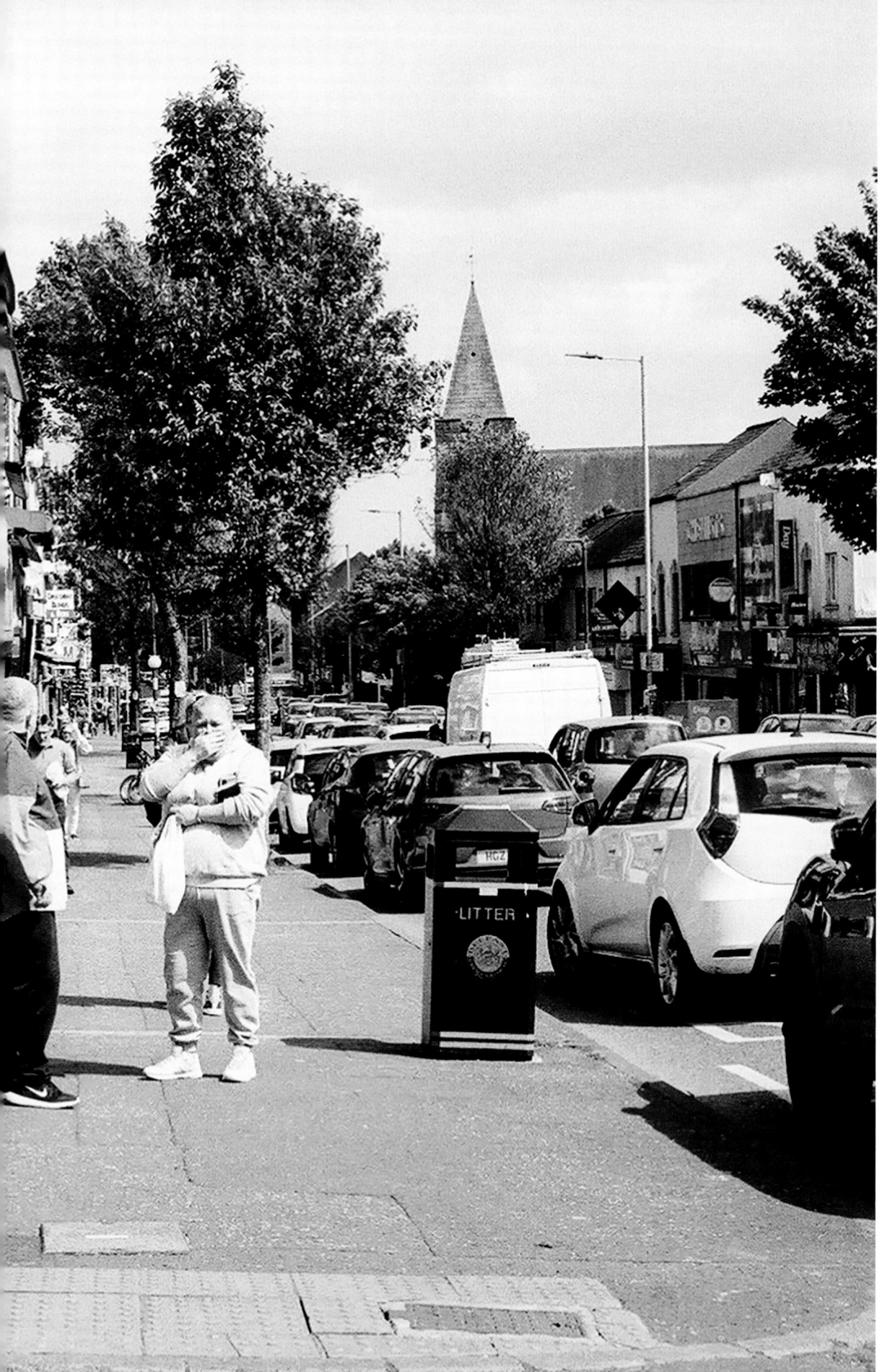

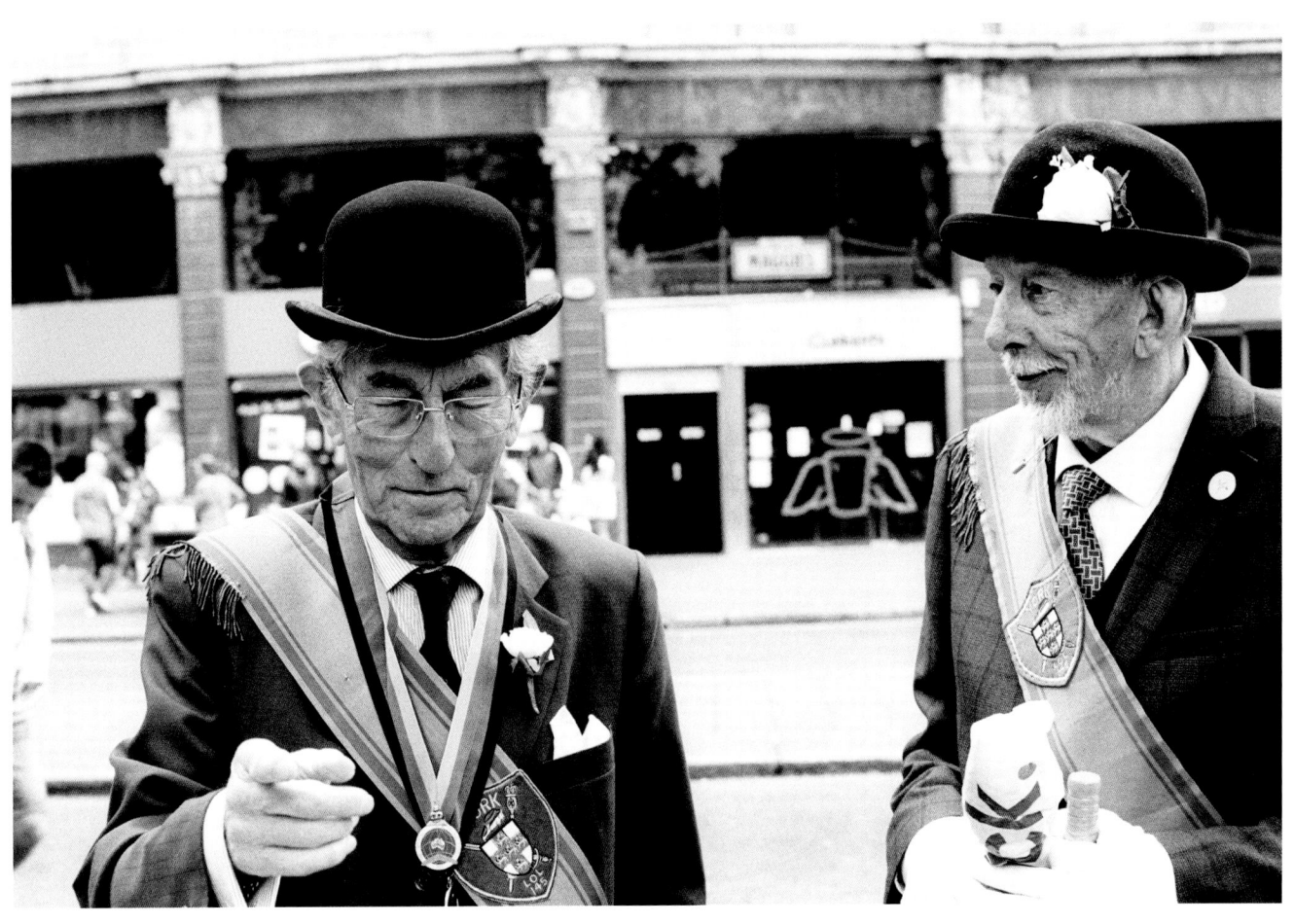

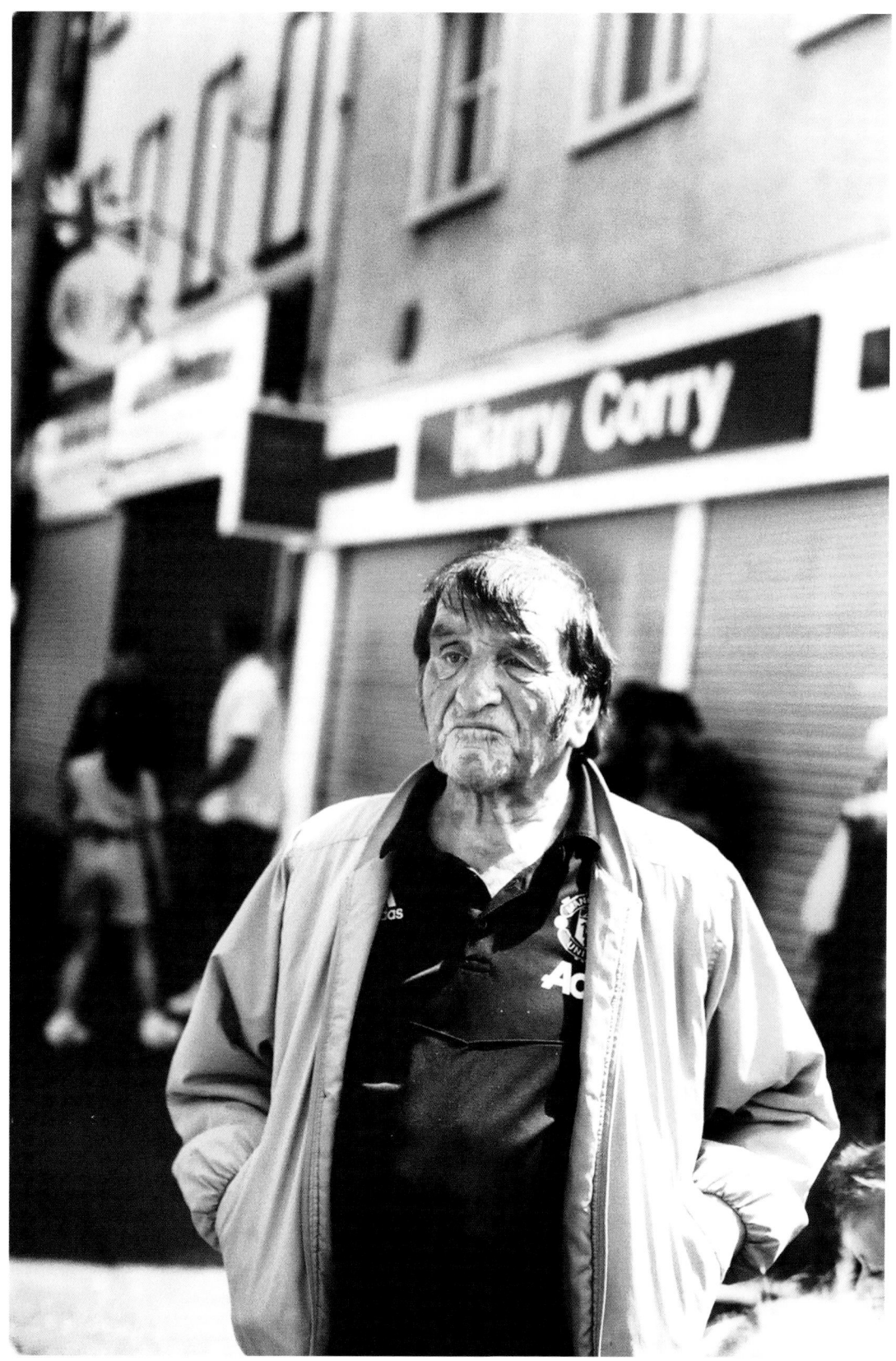

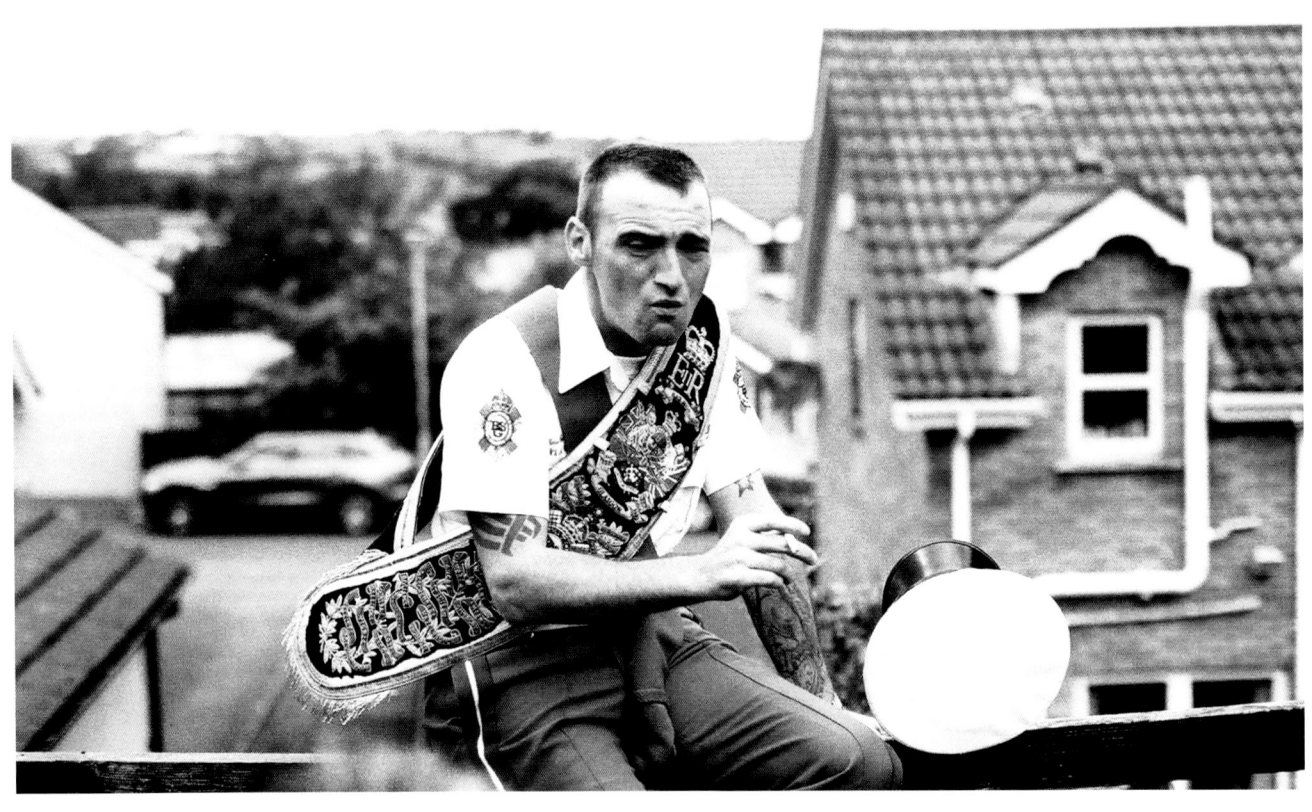

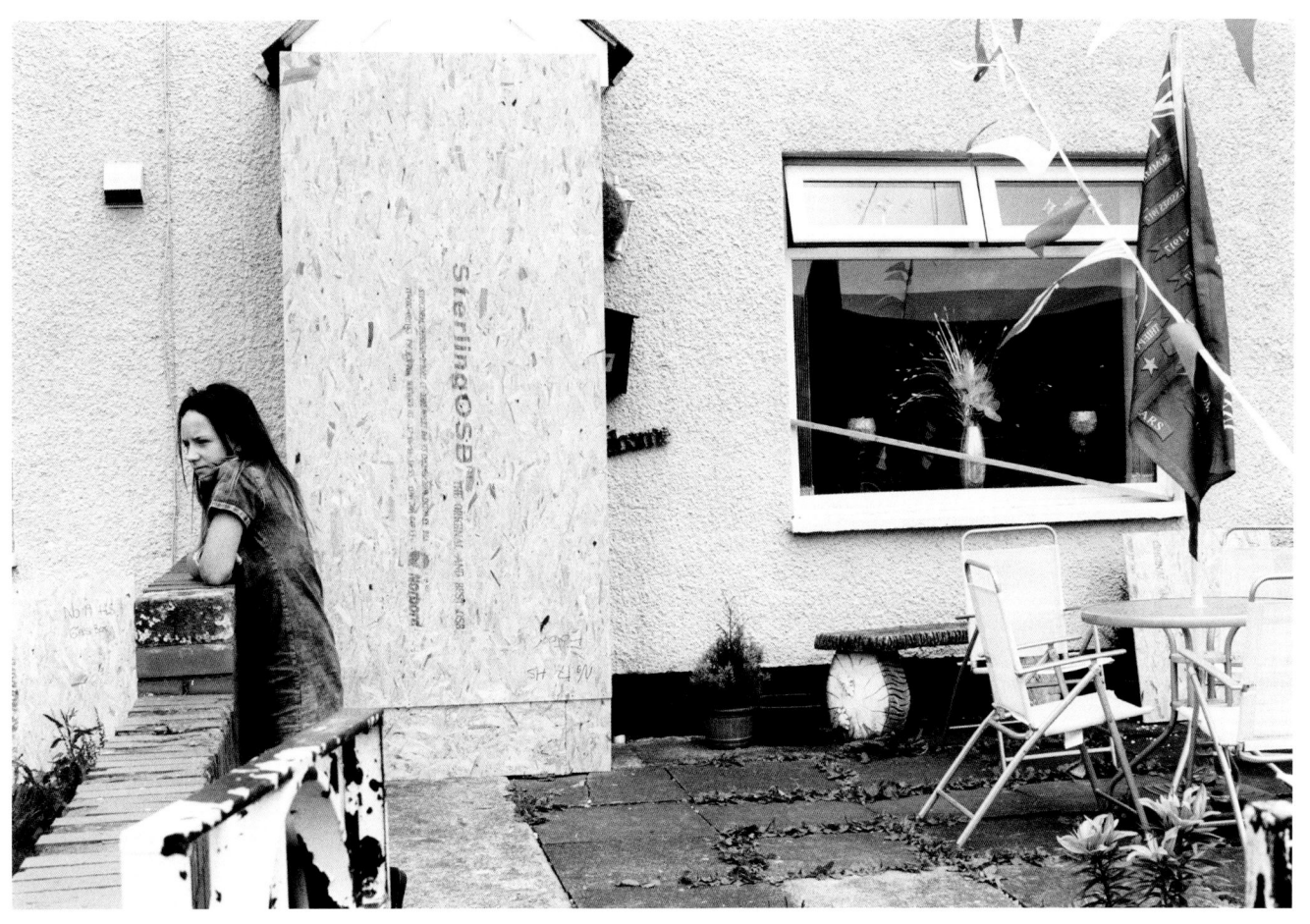

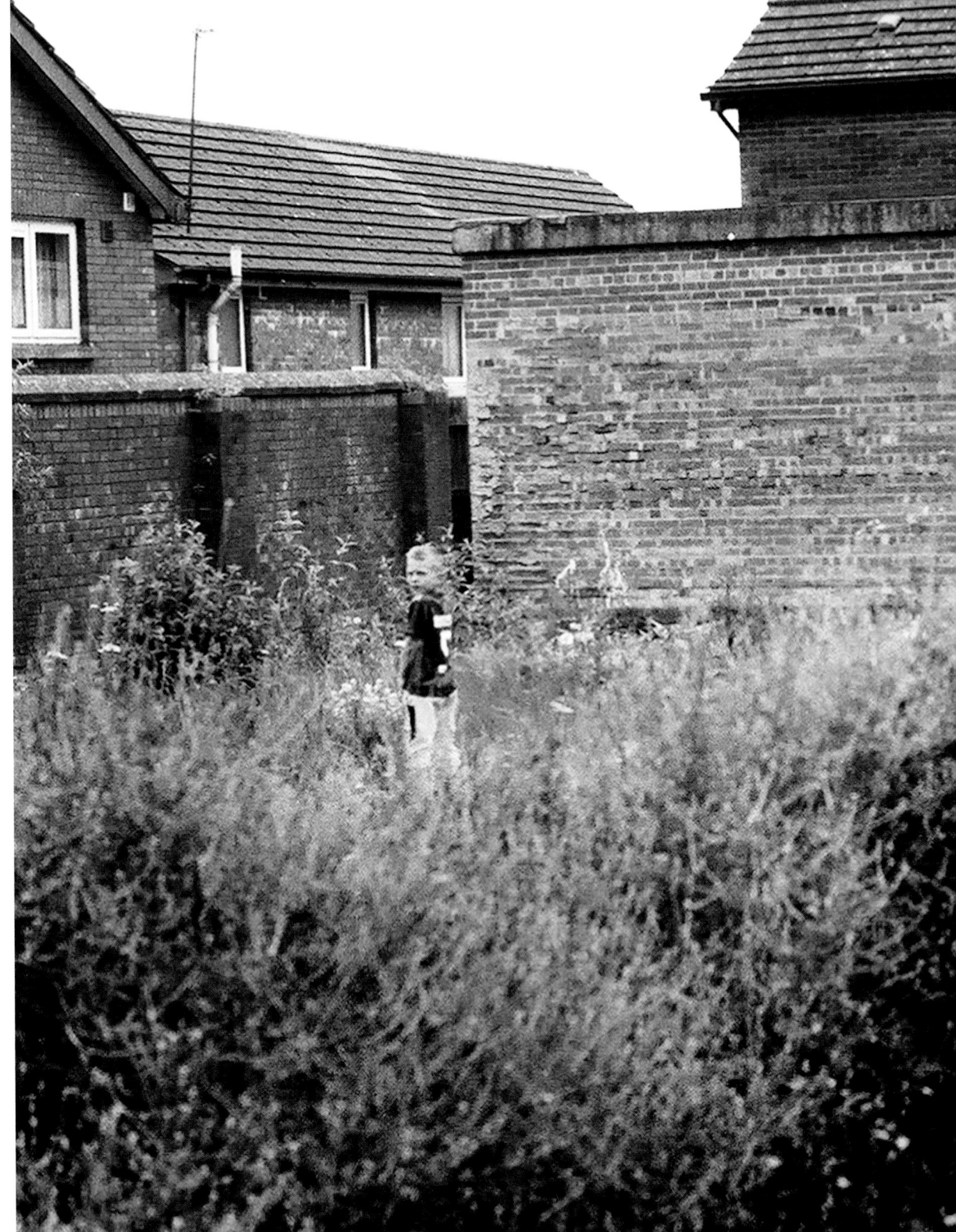

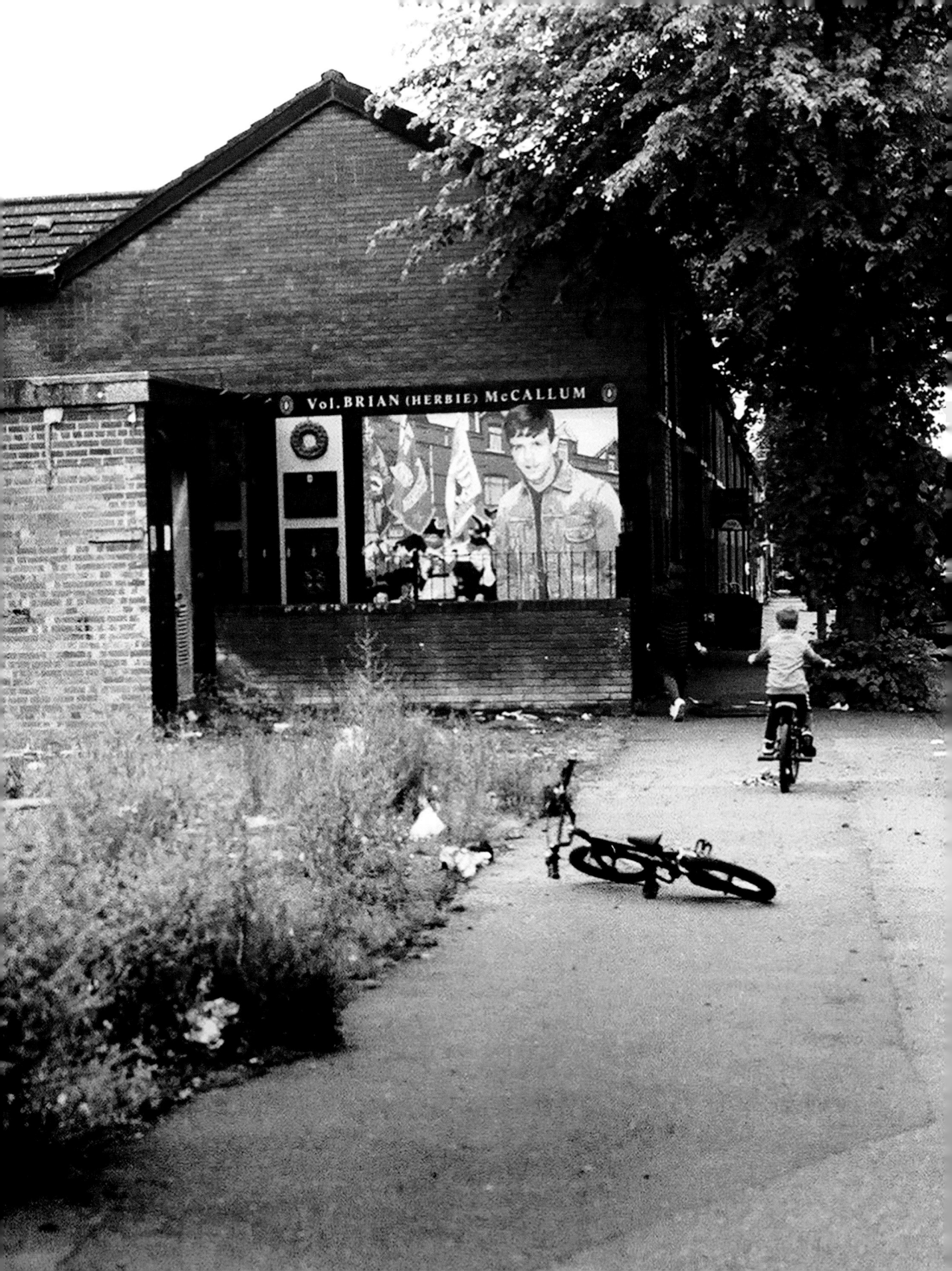

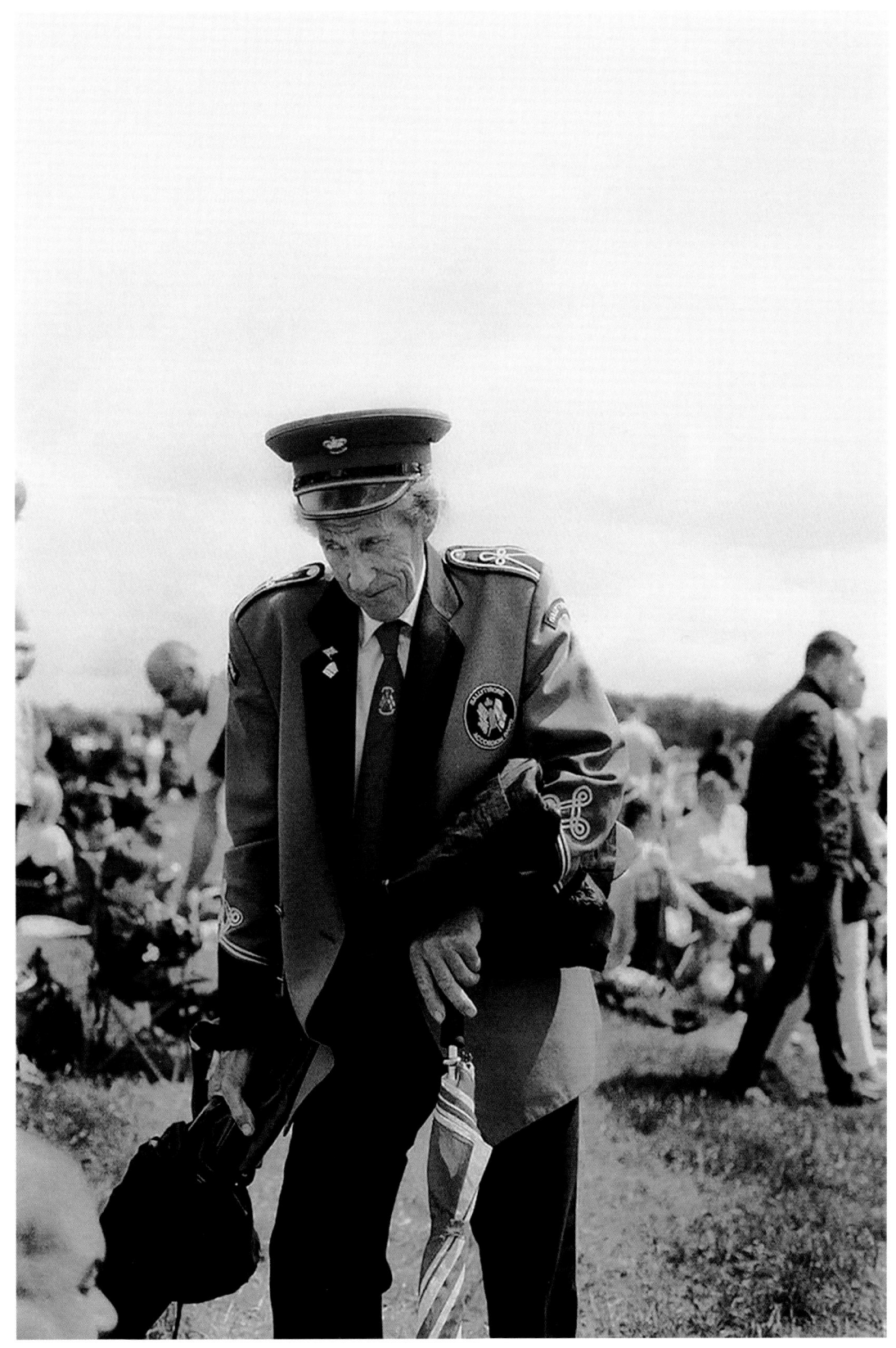

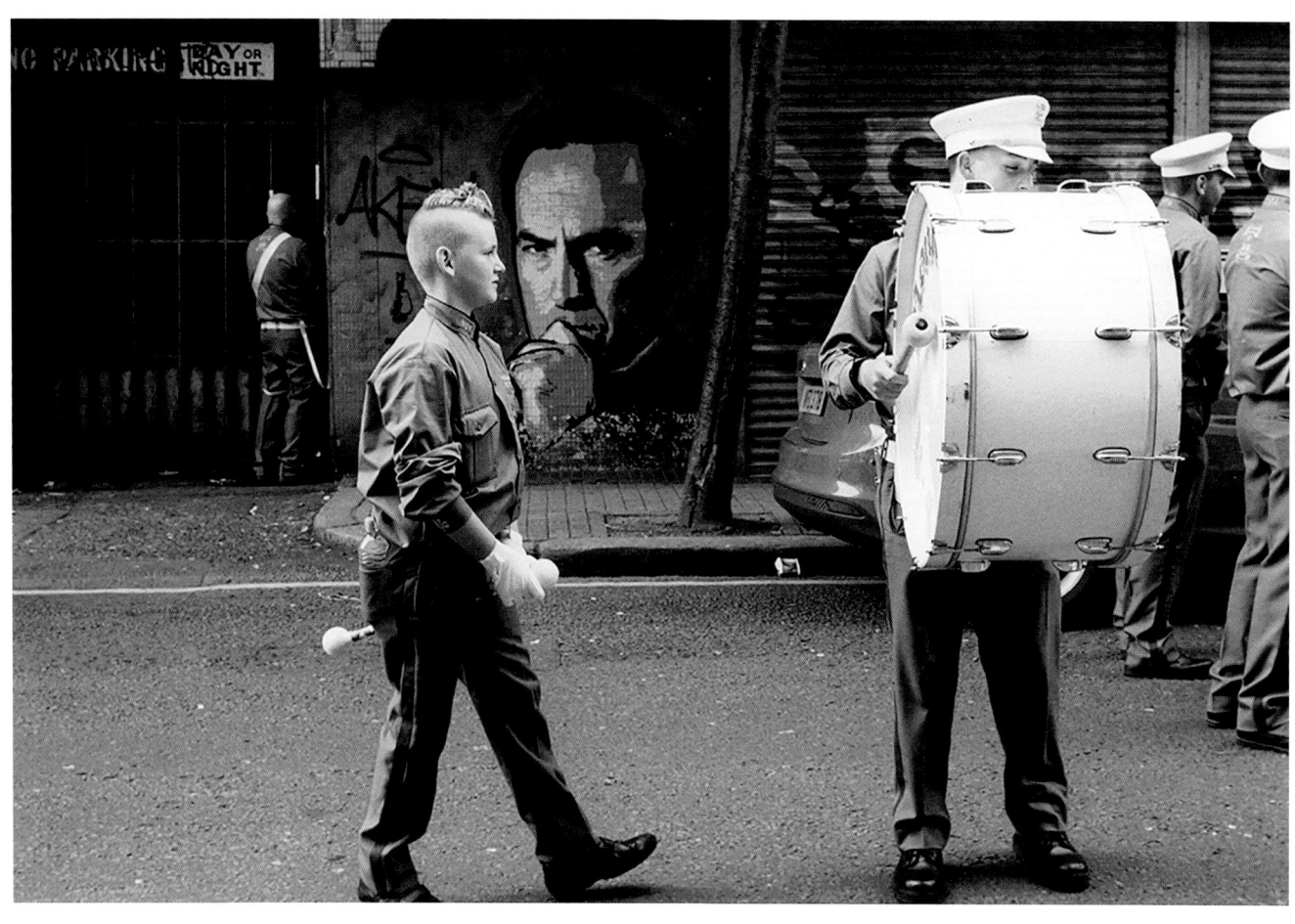

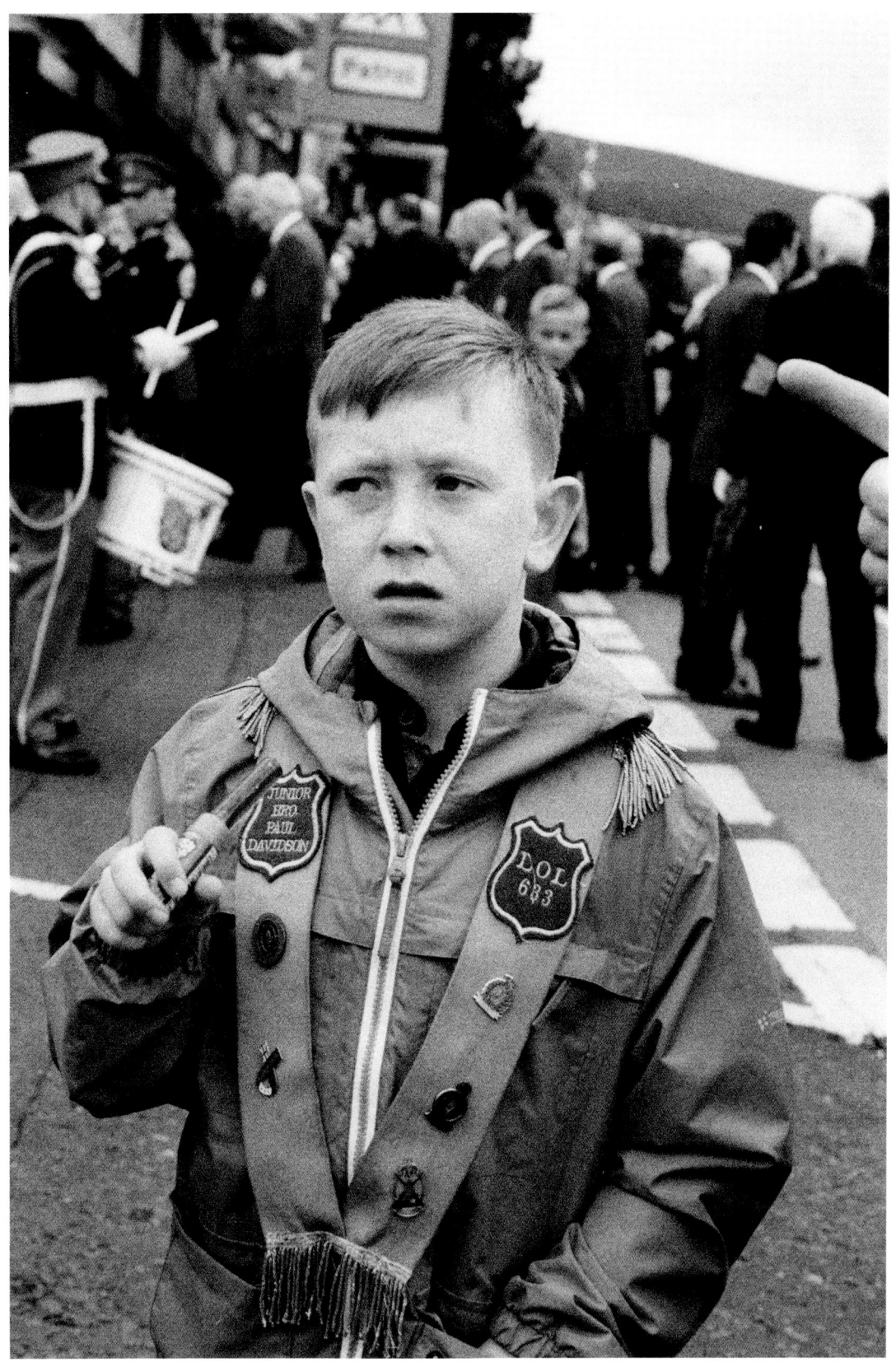

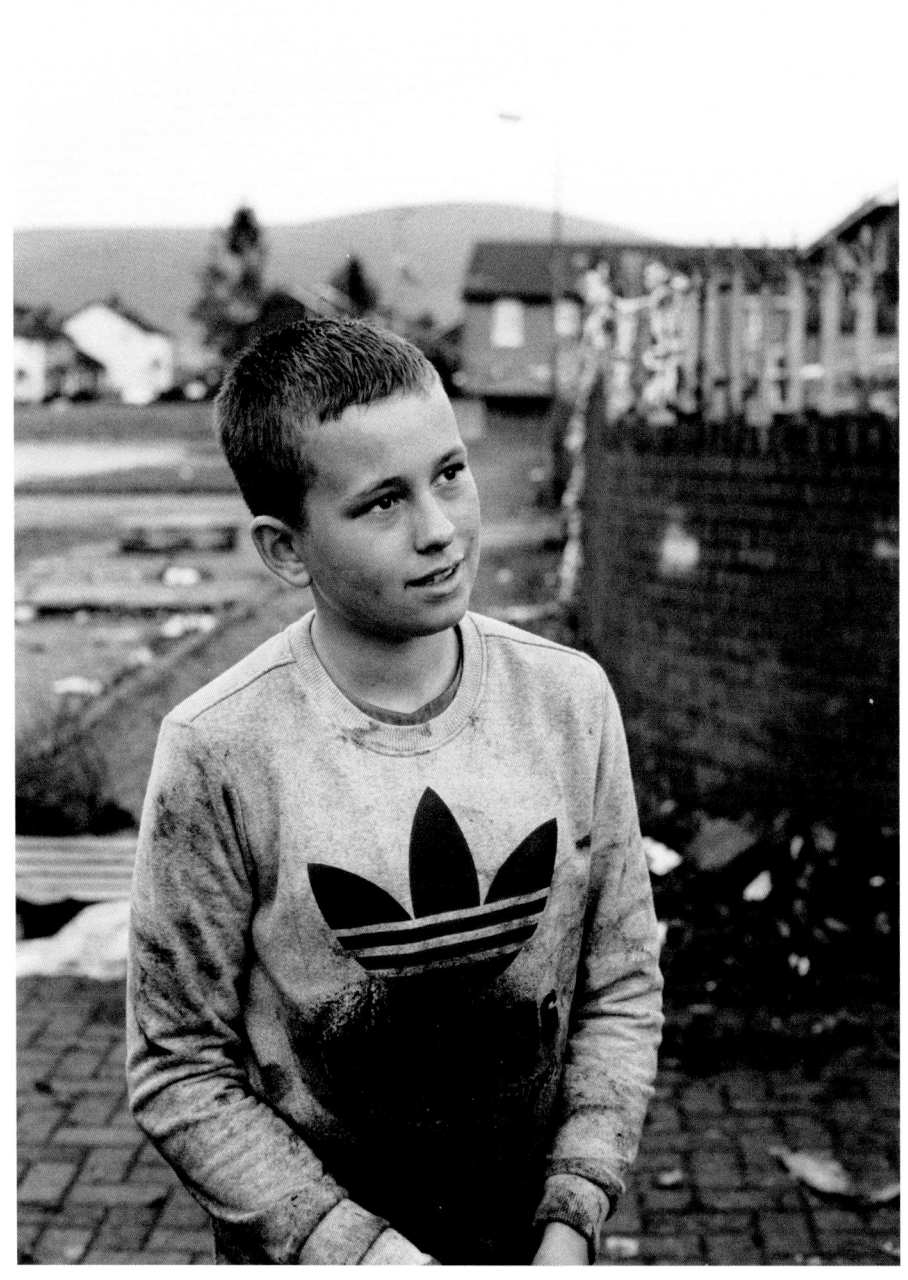

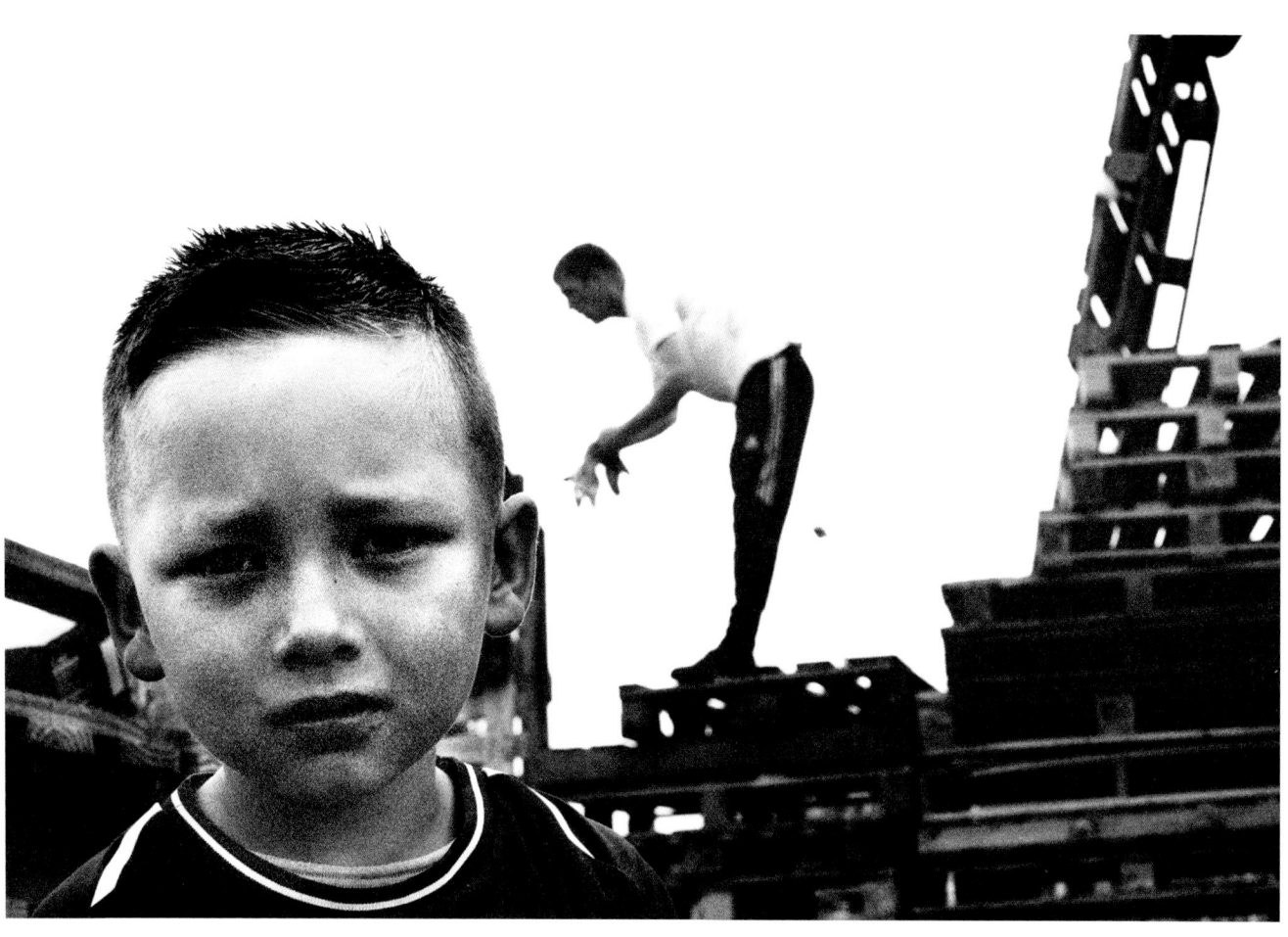

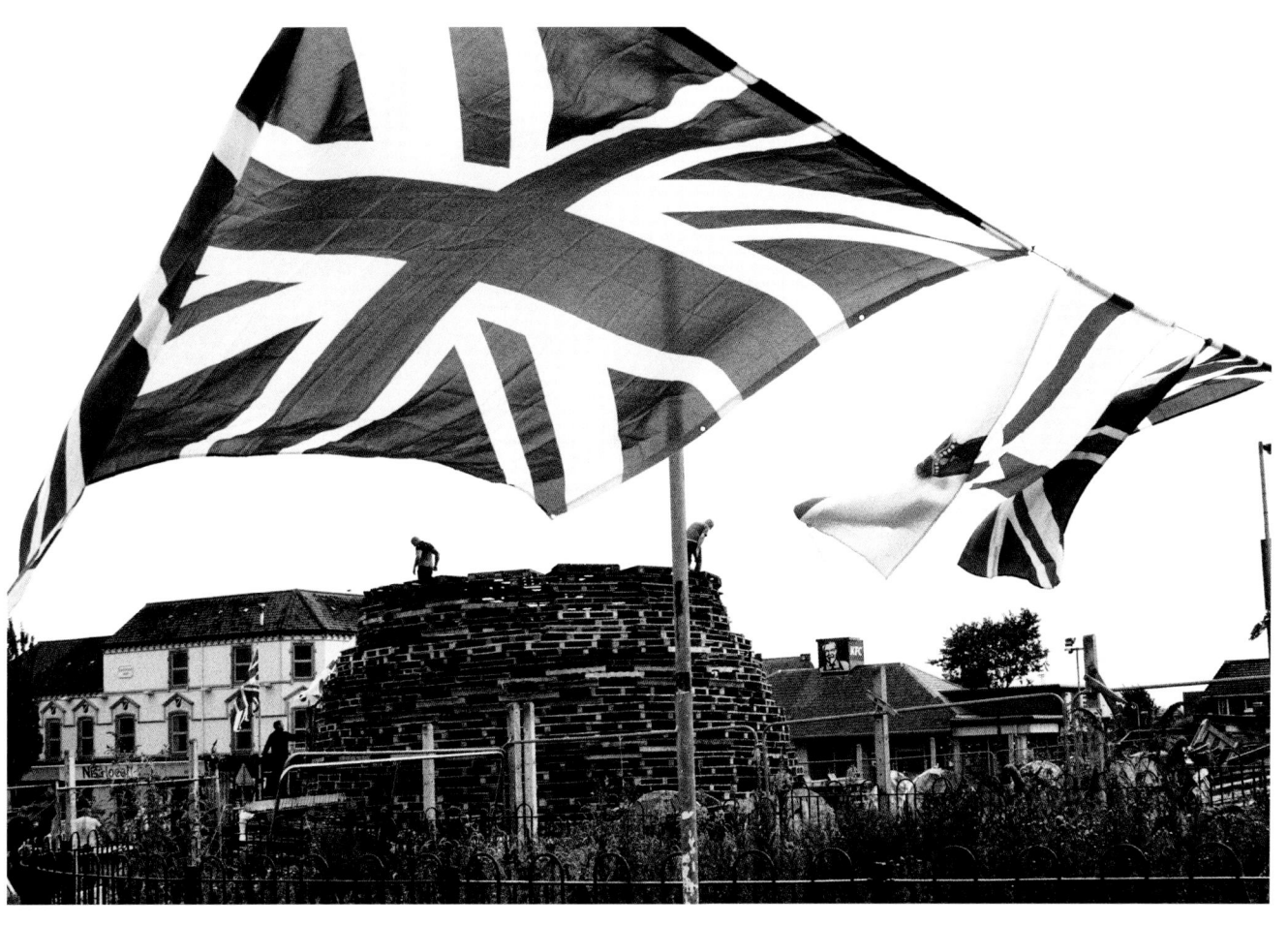

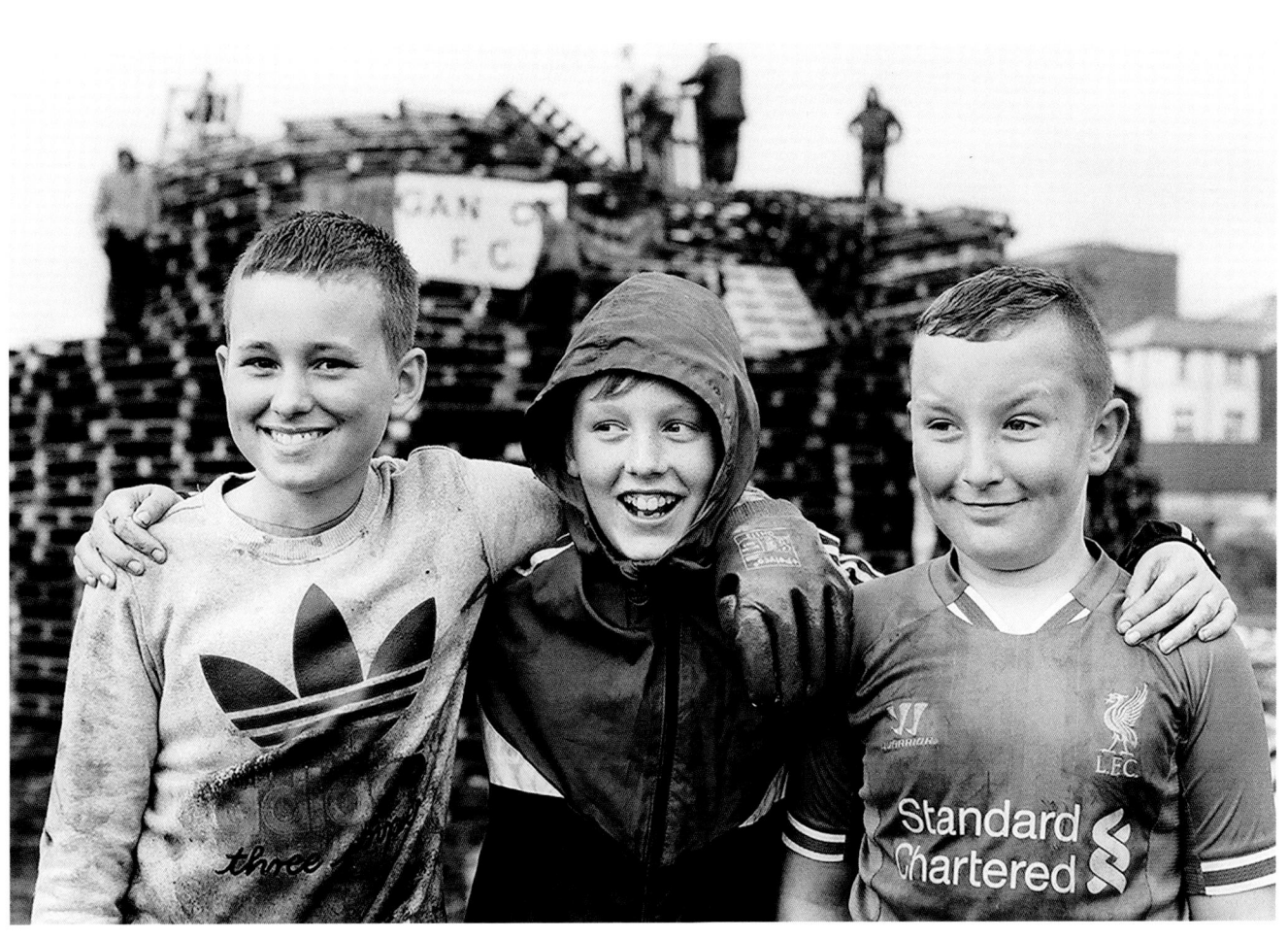

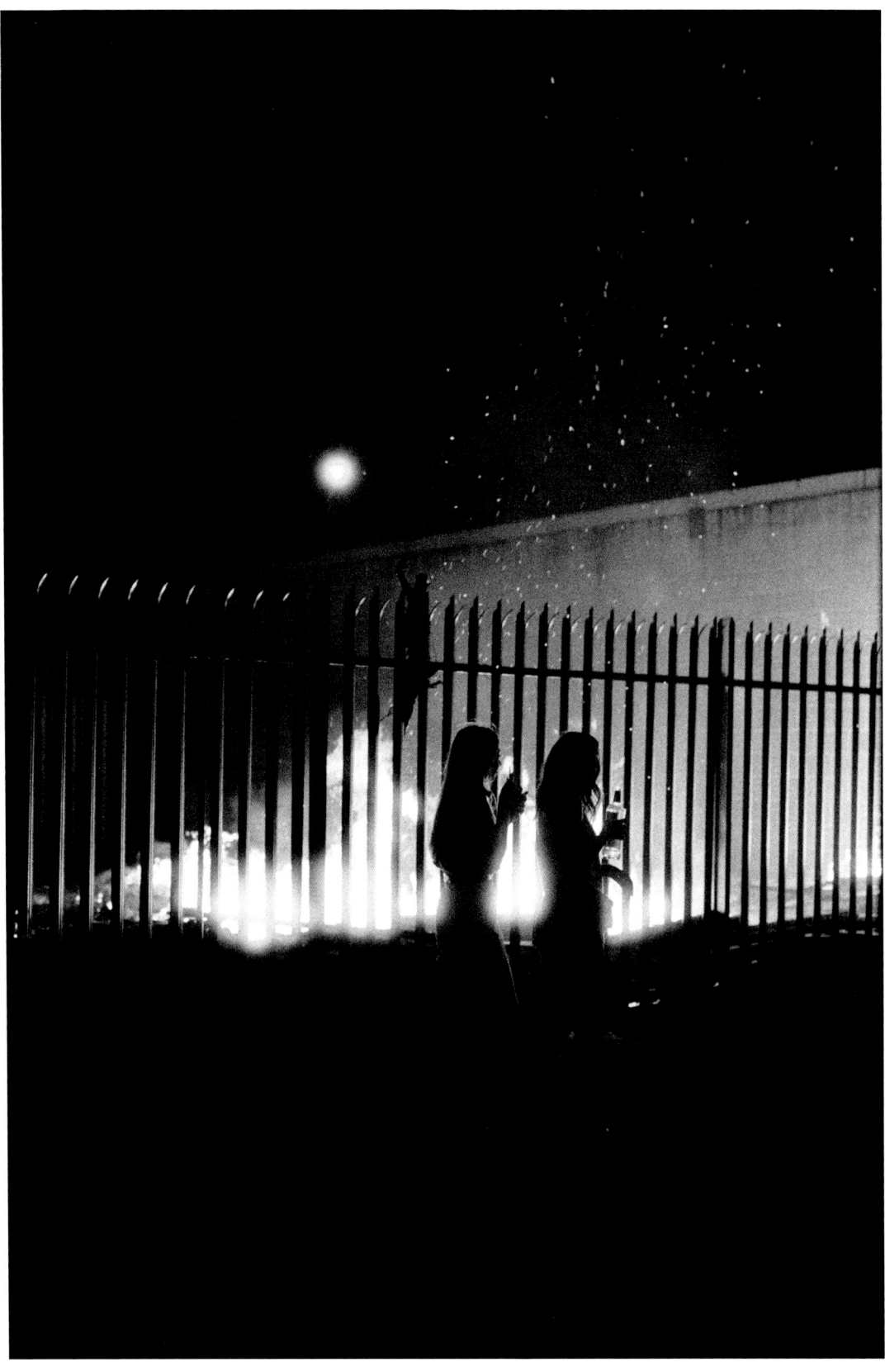

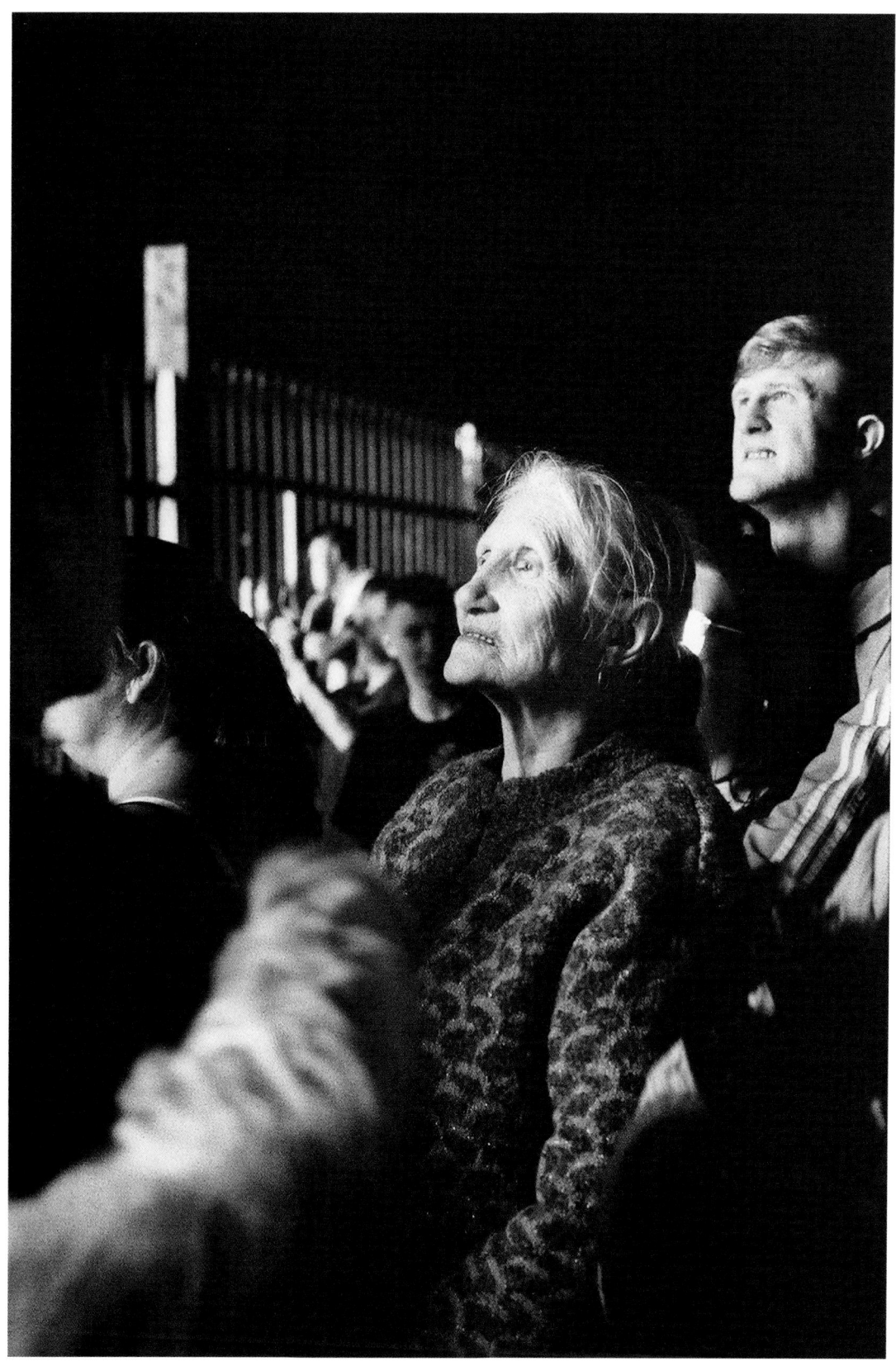

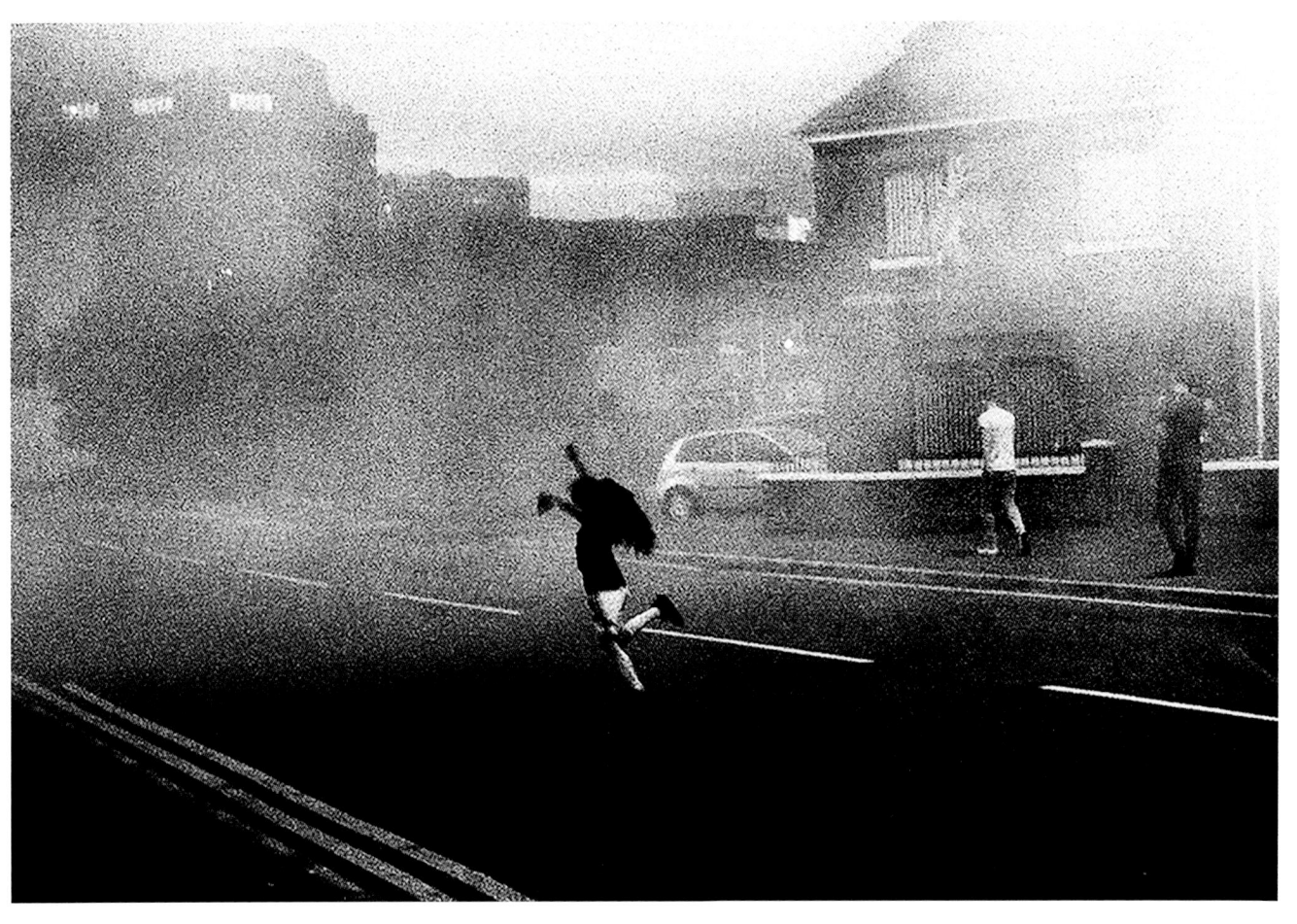

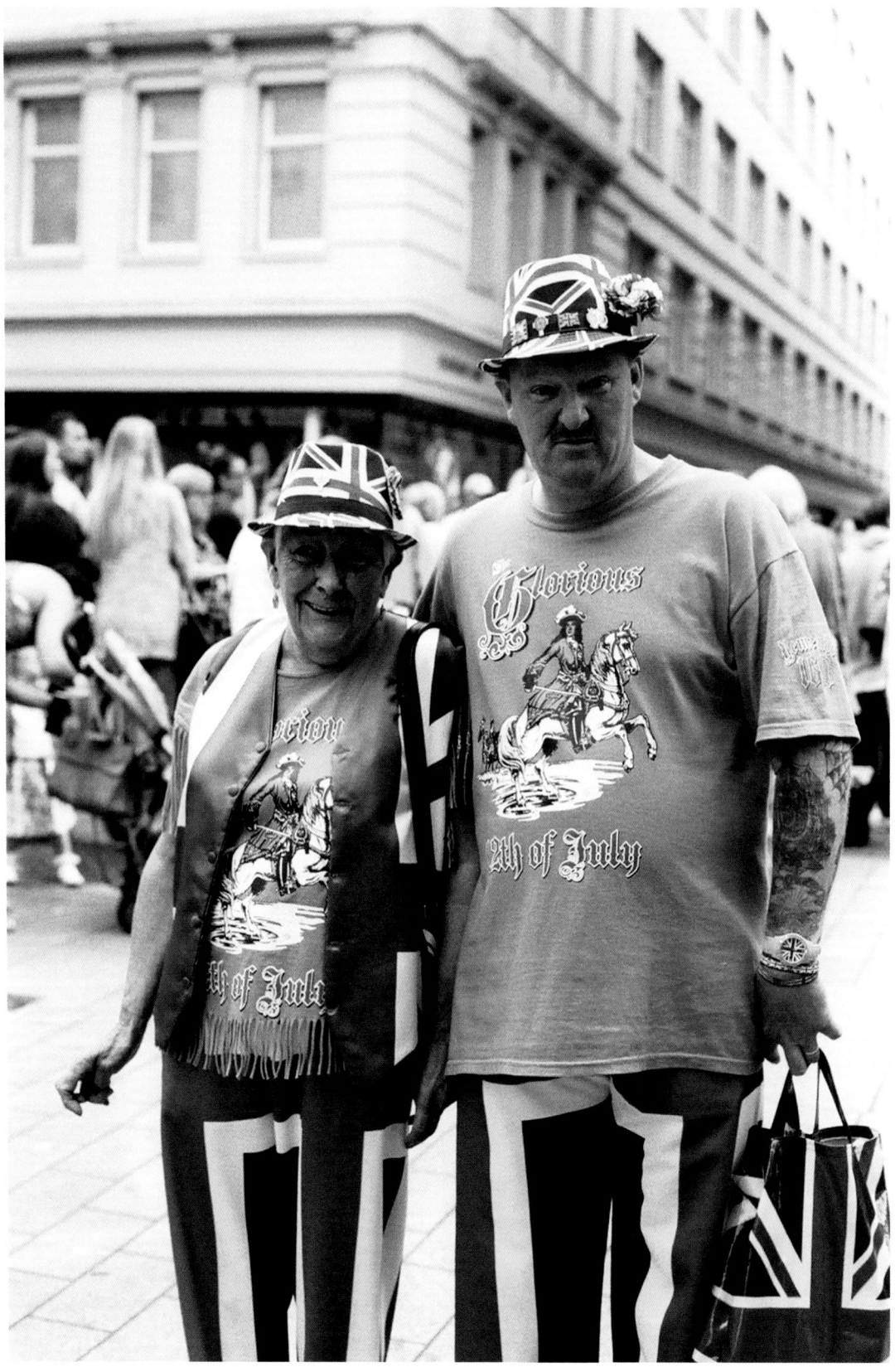

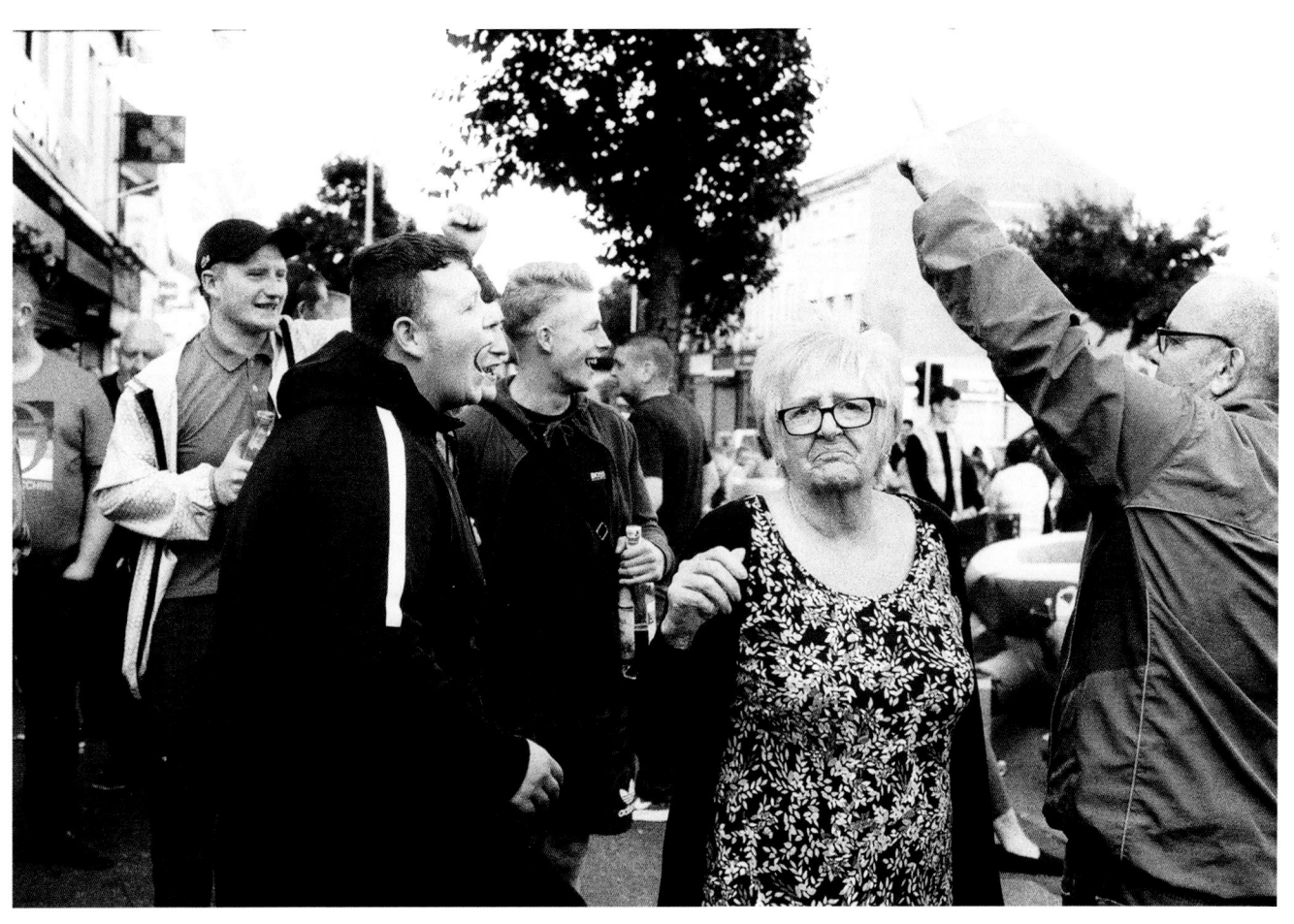

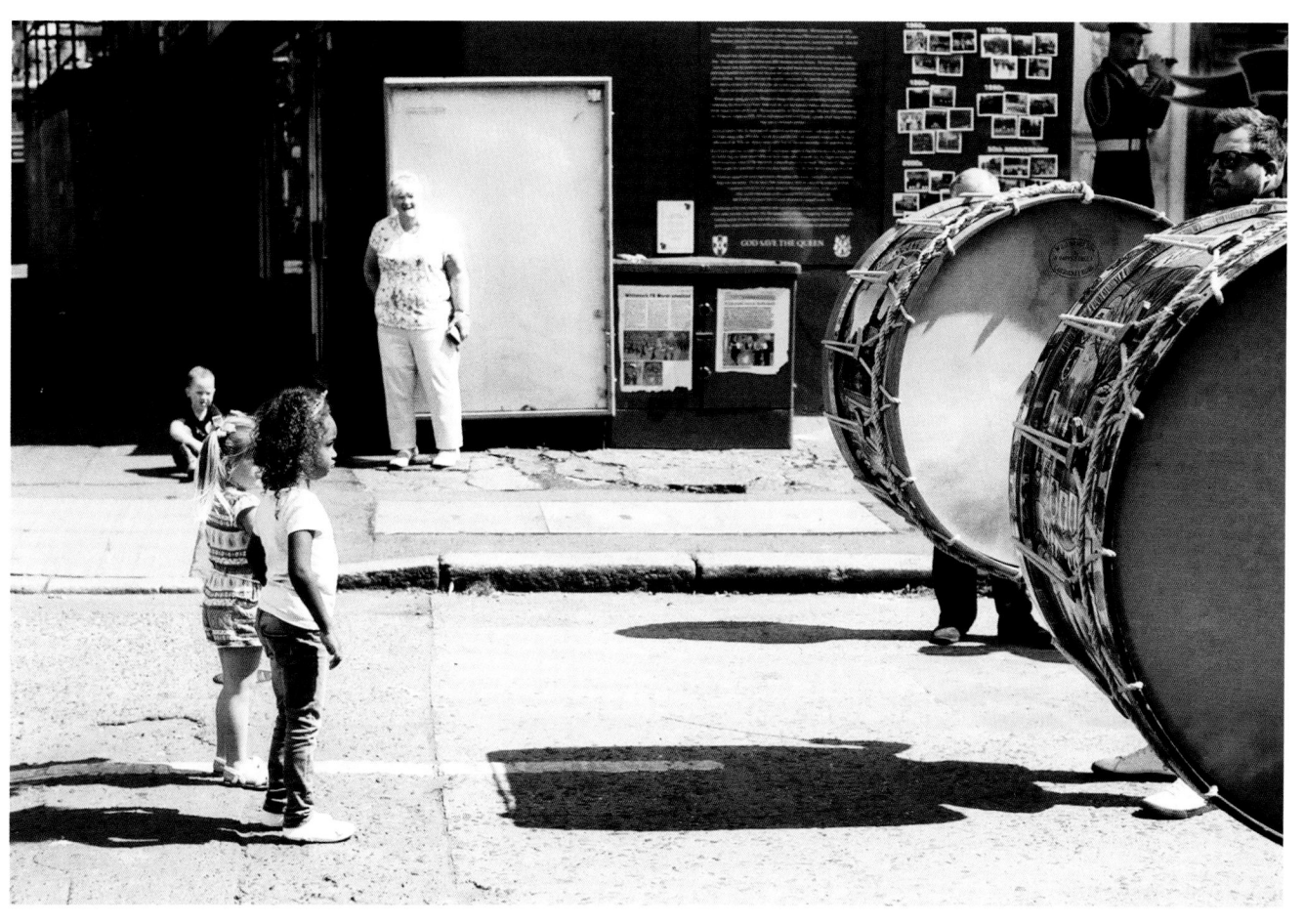

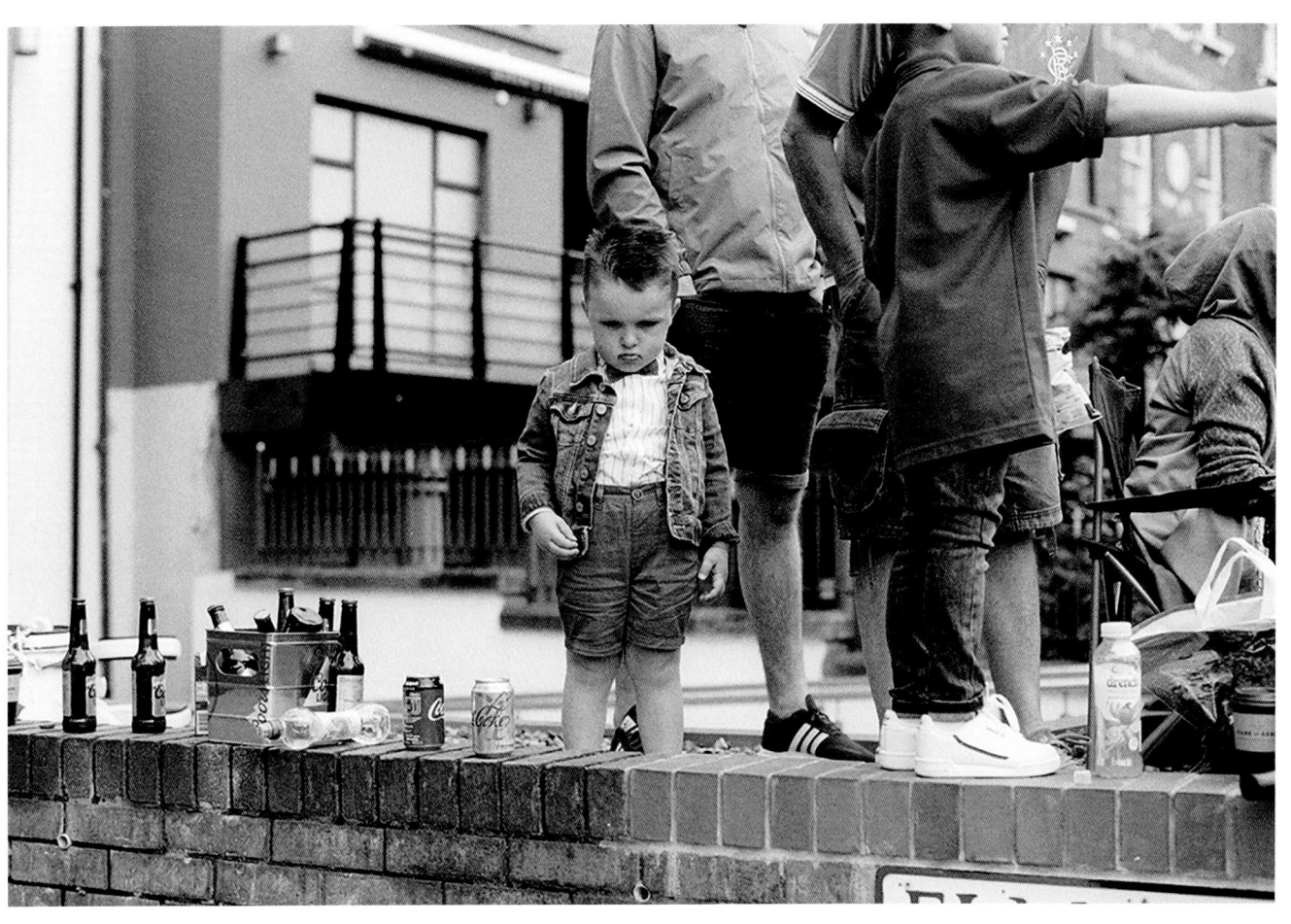

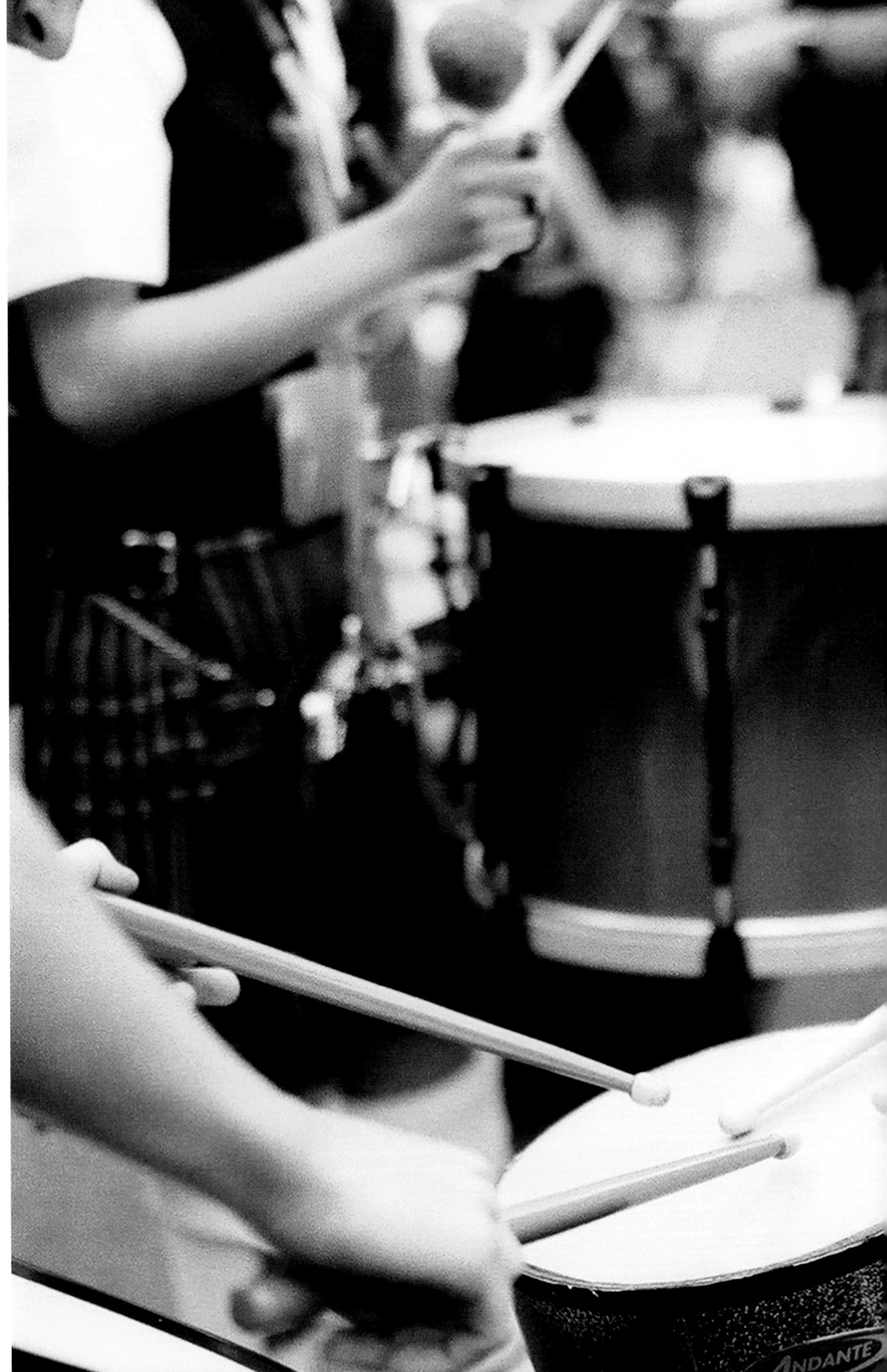

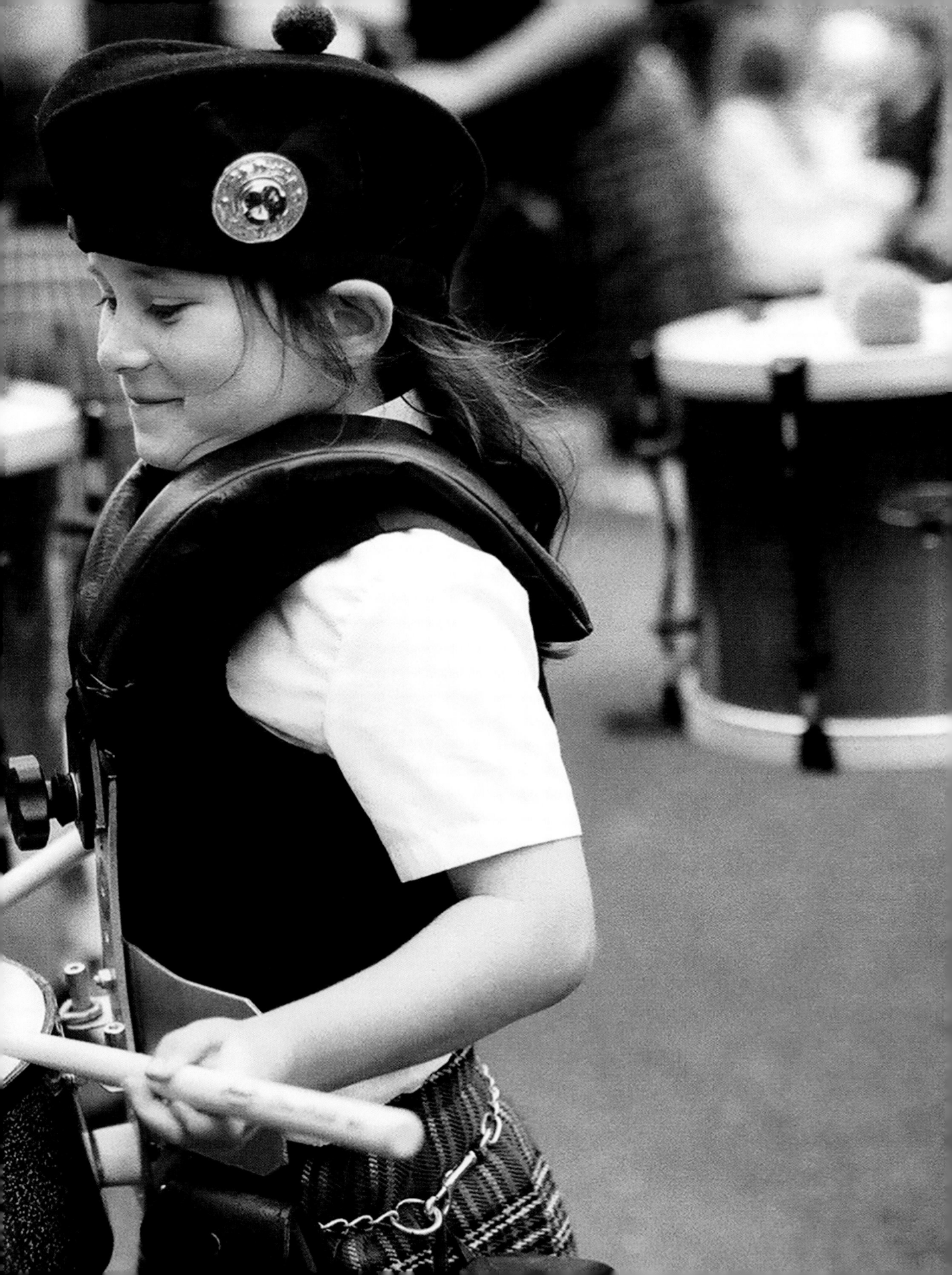

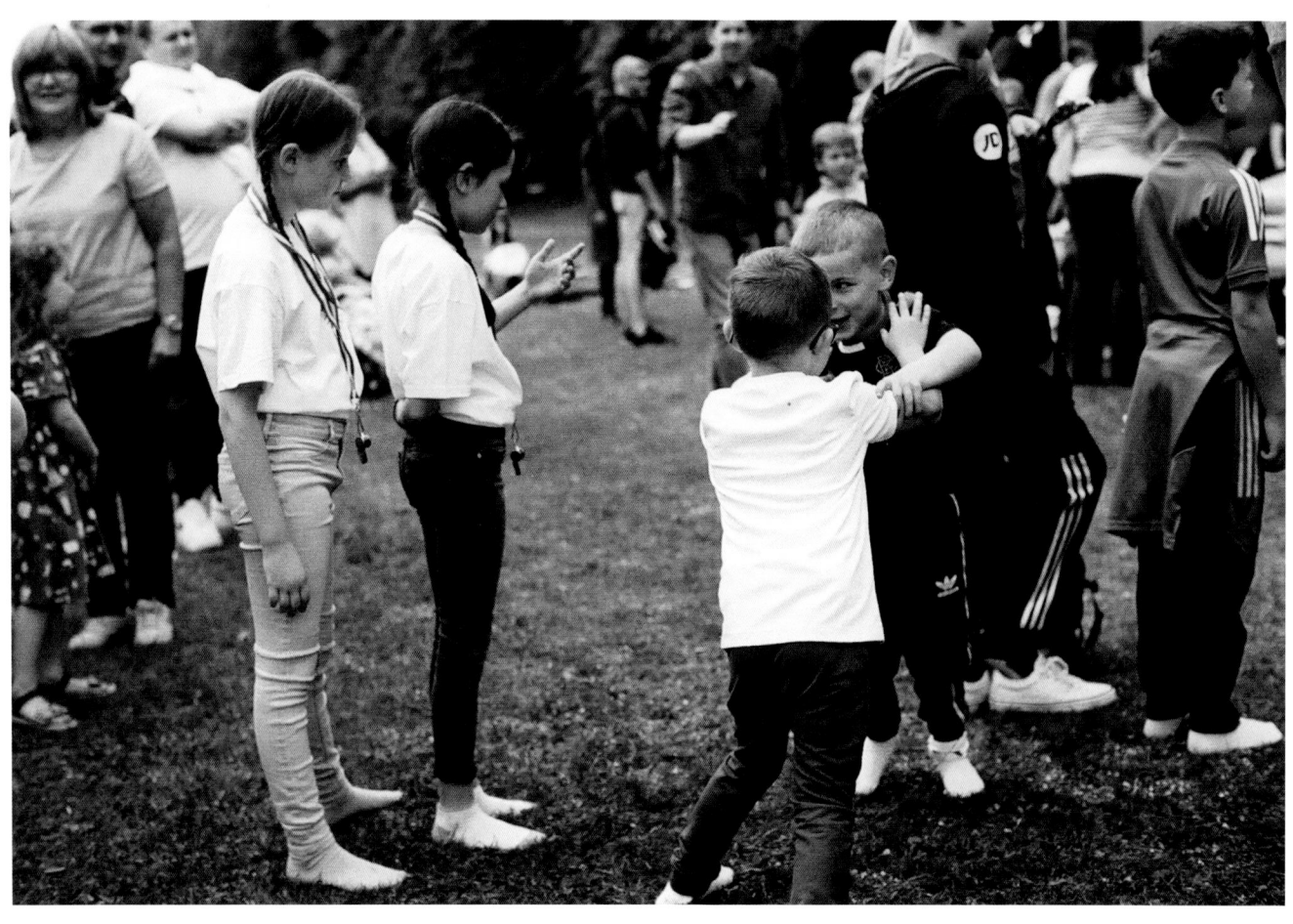

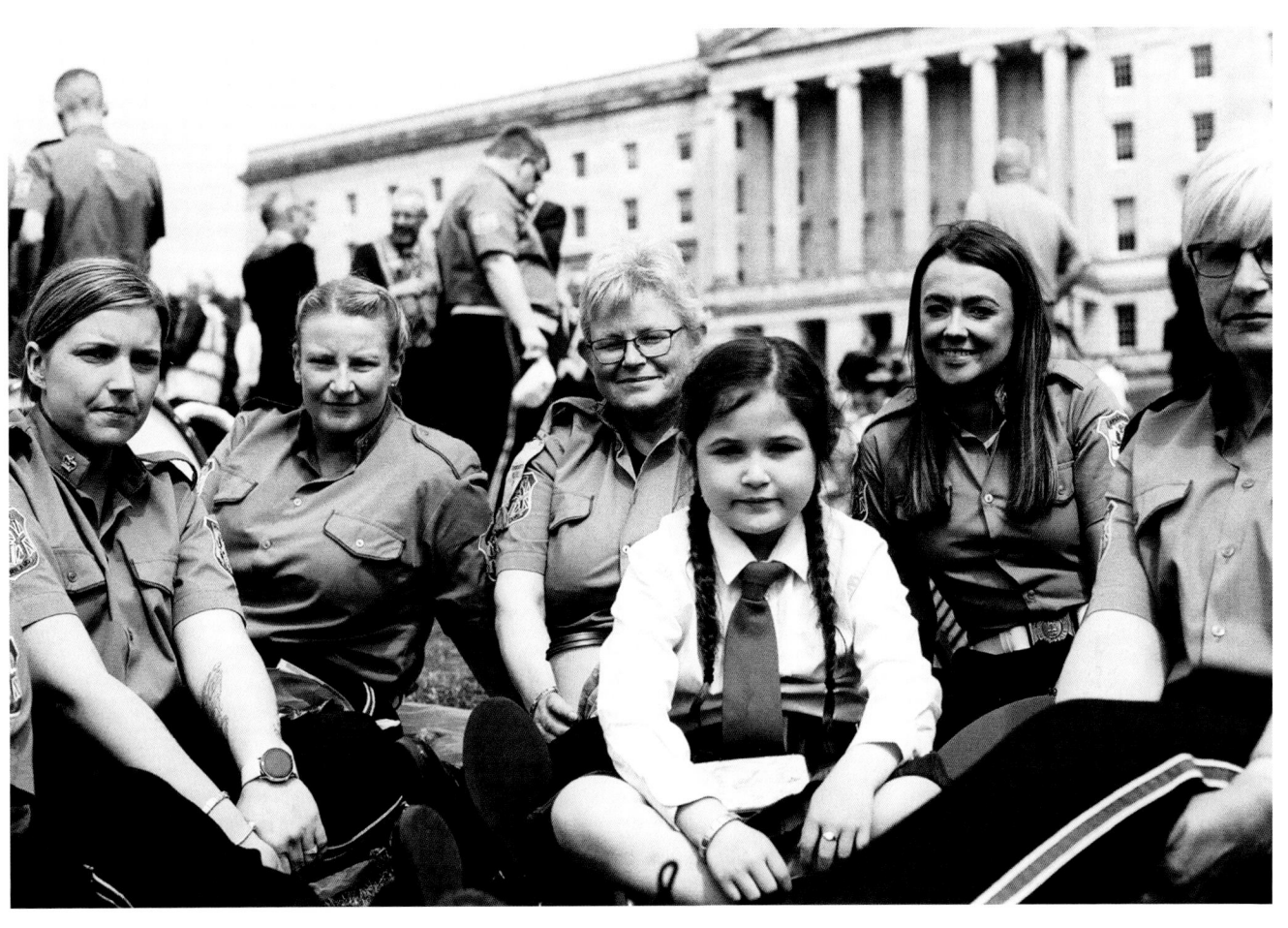

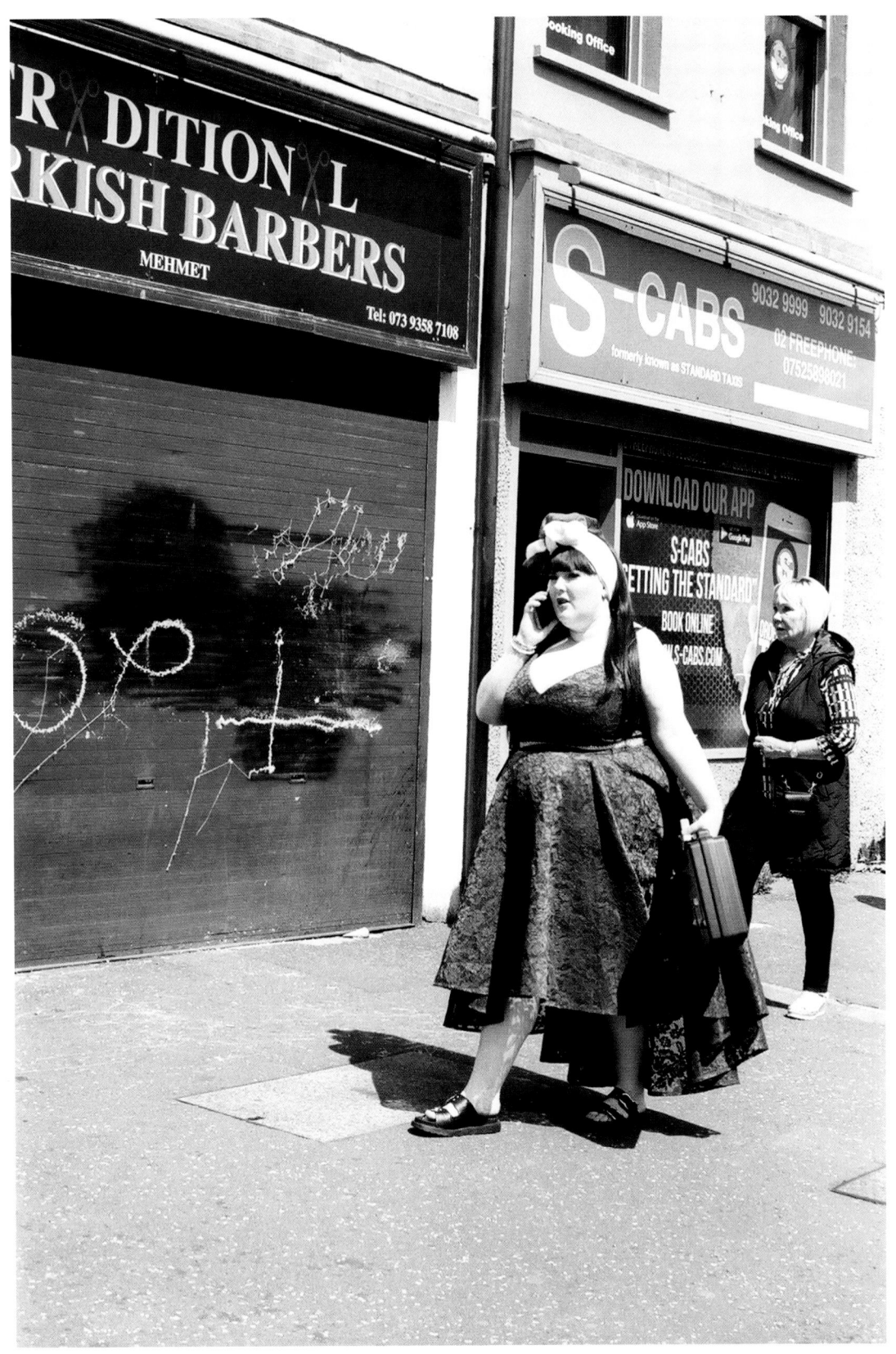

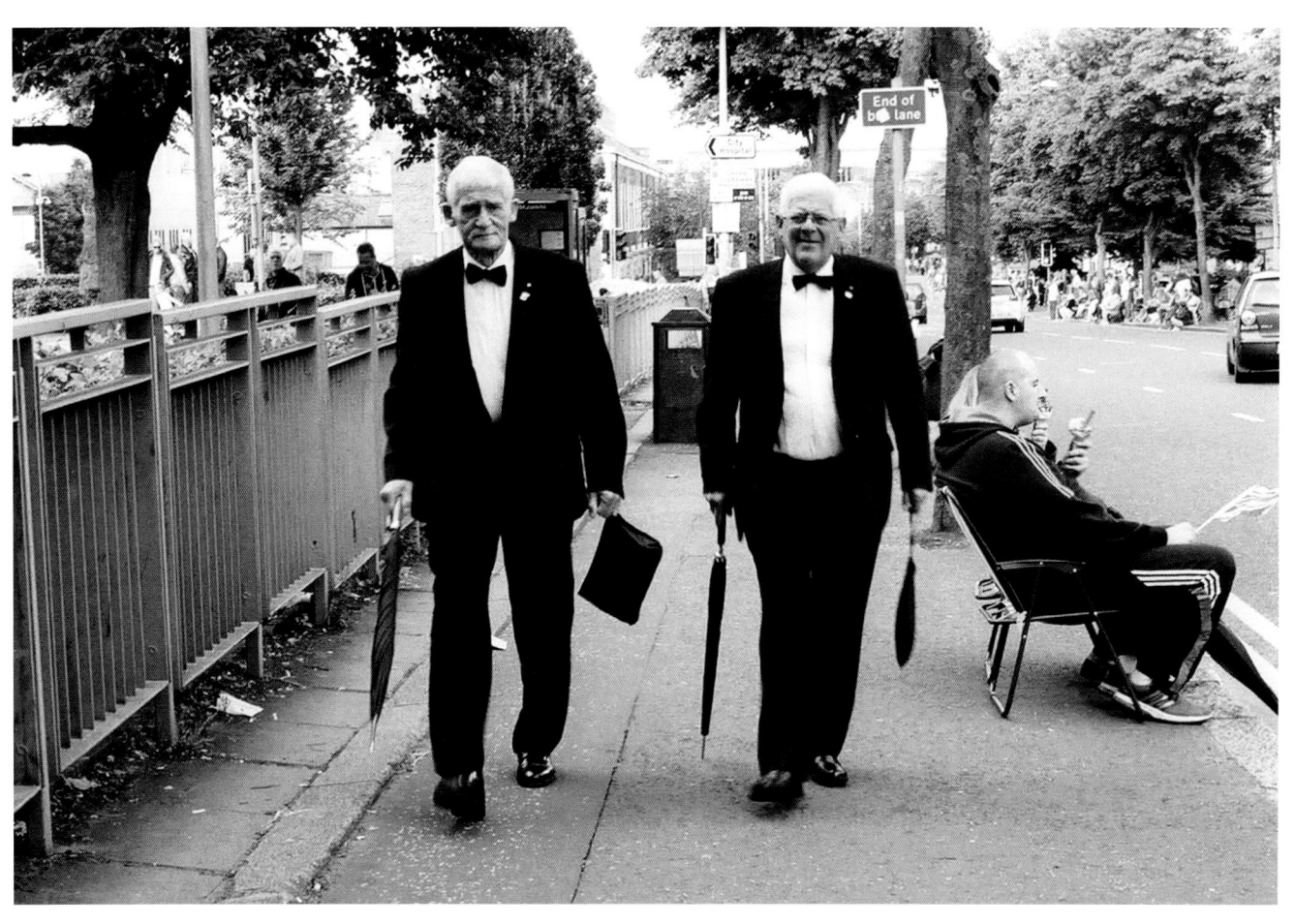

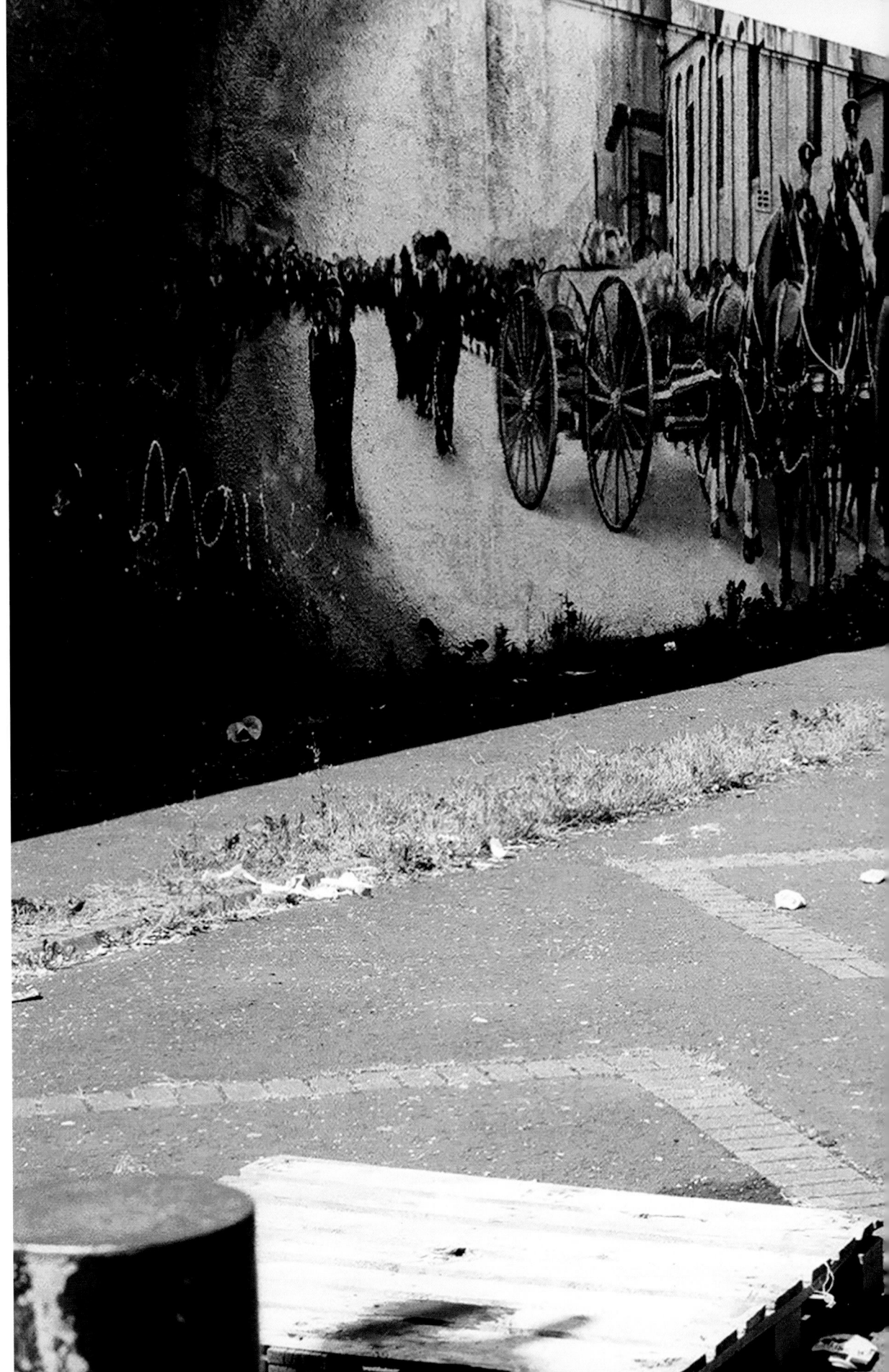

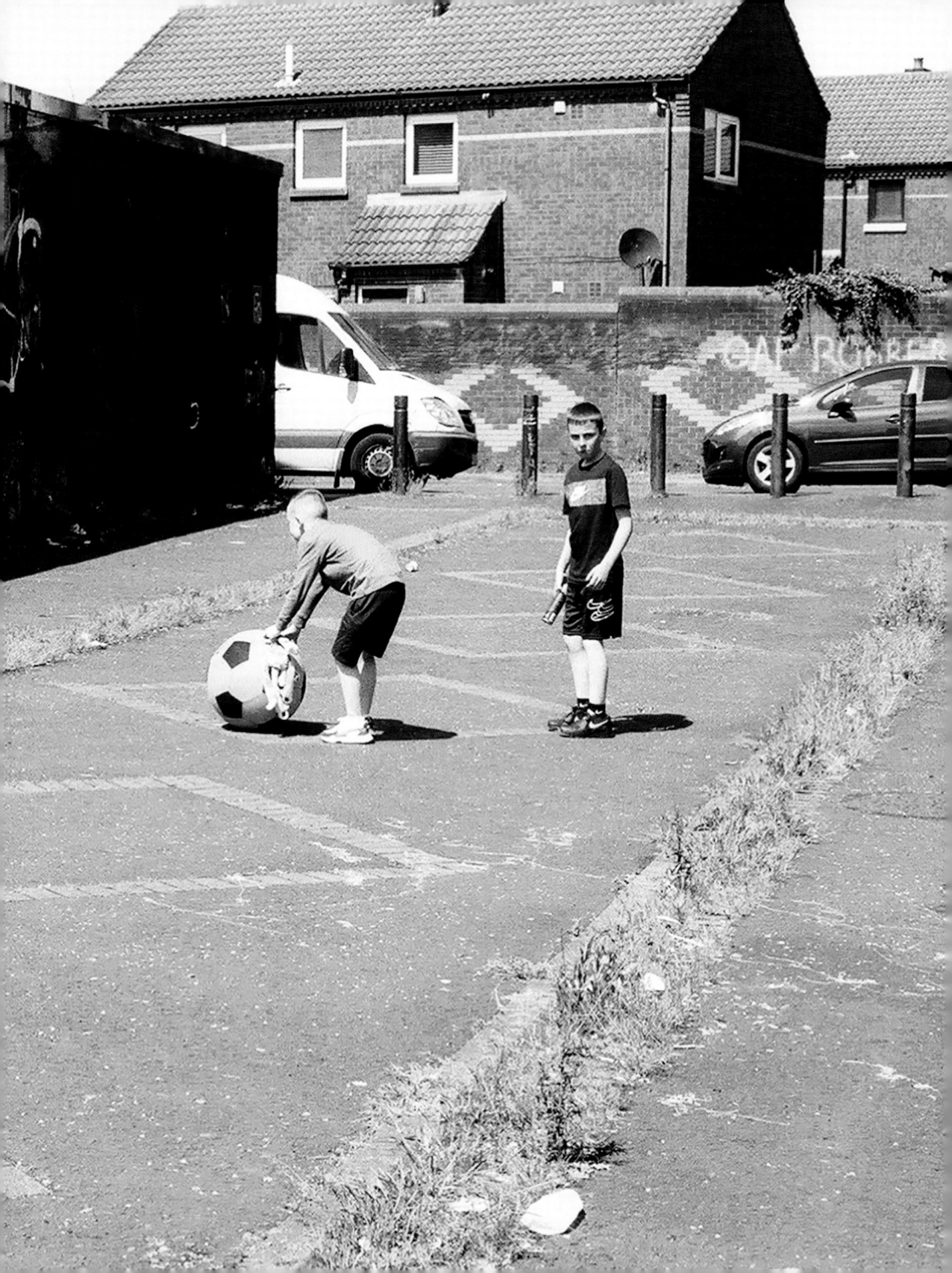

ACKNOWLEDGMENTS

Thank you to the people of the Shankill, particularly William Mitchell, Jackie Redpath, Rev. Jack Lamb, and Julie Davidson and her family. Thanks also to David Torrans, owner of No Alibis bookstore.

My thanks also to Jason Langer, Matthew Pappas, my Photo Sisters, and my husband, David, without whom I would never have visited the Shankill in the first place, and whose endless patience has seen me through to the end.

Lastly, thanks to Daylight Books for believing in this project.